INVISIBLE COMPANIONS

INVISIBLE COMPANIONS

Encounters with Imaginary Friends,
Gods, Ancestors, and Angels

J. Bradley Wigger

STANFORD UNIVERSITY PRESS · STANFORD, CALIFORNIA

STANFORD UNIVERSITY PRESS

Stanford, California

©2019 by the Board of Trustees of the Leland Stanford Junior University.
All rights reserved.

Printed in the United States of America on acid-free, archival-quality paper

Library of Congress Cataloging-in-Publication Data

Names: Wigger, J. Bradley, author.

Title: Invisible companions : encounters with imaginary friends, gods, ancestors, and angels / J. Bradley Wigger.

Description: Stanford, California : Stanford University Press, 2019. | Includes bibliographical references and index.

Identifiers: LCCN 2018045204 | ISBN 9781503609112 (cloth : alk. paper) | ISBN 9781503609181 (epub)

Subjects: LCSH: Imaginary companions—Religious aspects—Cross-cultural studies. | Imagination—Religious aspects—Cross-cultural studies. | Imagination in children—Cross-cultural studies.

Classification: LCC BL65.I427 W54 2019 | DDC 153.3—dc23

LC record available at https://lccn.loc.gov/2018045204

Cover design: Rob Ehle

Cover art: (photo) DigitalGrill | iStockphoto; (drawing) *Dino*, by "Kent"

Text design: Kevin Barrett Kane

Typeset at Stanford University Press in 11.5/16 Sabon

To Crystal

CONTENTS

INVISIBLE COMPANIONS

SEE-THROUGH KNOWING

*Alice started to her feet, for it flashed across her
mind that she had never before seen a rabbit with
either a waistcoat-pocket, or a watch to take out of
it, and burning with curiosity, she ran across the
field after it.*

—LEWIS CARROLL

I SENT MY DAUGHTER an email from the Dominican Republic and
she was thrilled.

> *Cora,*
>
> *We interviewed today—several children had IFs. One was of a girl, 7,
who was named "Crystal"!*

It seemed I had found Cora's long-lost invisible friend, Crystal,
twenty years after she'd gone missing. She now kept company with a
seven-year-old girl named Maria living in Santo Domingo. Crystal spoke
Spanish and according to Maria spelled her name with an *i* instead of
the *y*—Cristal. But the meaning remains the same: Fine glass. Transparent. See-through.

The adventures with invisible friends described in this book began a long
way from the lush heat of the Caribbean, on the icy shores of Lake Winnebago in Oshkosh, Wisconsin, twenty-two years earlier. I was cleaning
up after lunch, and I heard Cora say something. "What was that?" I asked.

No response.

"Cora?" She was ignoring me and still talking. "Honey?" I whispered this time—a little parenting trick I learned to sneak under kids' attention when they are playing—"Who are you talking to?"

She paused, then turned and answered, "Crystal."

"Oh," I said in full voice, startled by how real the name made her invisible friend. And I let the two of them play as I finished the dishes.

Cora was three years old at the time, but we never thought to ask how old Crystal was. Though Cora had plenty of friends—the kind we could see—this was the first and only one of the invisible type I had ever met. Neither my wife, Jane, nor I had had invisible friends as far as either of us knows, nor had Cora's older brother David (though he did hang with the *Teenage Mutant Ninja Turtles* a lot). This world of transparent friends was new.

Crystal turned out to have a last name too, Malaver. Sometimes Cora pronounced a "t" at the end, making it Malavert; sometimes she did not. We knew no Crystals or Malaver(t)s, so the source of the name has always been a puzzle. I was struck at the time, though, and still am, at the see-through character of the name, Crystal, as if a three-year-old were creating the perfect pun for an invisible friend.

Crystal Malaver(t) stuck around for a couple of years, mostly to play with our daughter, though sometimes she would join us for an afternoon snack or a trip to the grocery store. "Would Crystal like a cookie?" Of course she would, Cora assured, taking an extra. "Oh, Crystal is going to the store too?" In this case I would buckle the invisible partner into a pretend car seat. Here was a wonderfully strange world in which the physical and imaginary blended to create a kind of living novel in our home, one full of settings, plots, and characters. The question is why.

An assumption I had early on was that Crystal, in addition to someone to play with, was a convenient scapegoat. One day, for example, I noticed near the garbage can some trash on the floor that had missed its target. "I bet Crystal did that," I said to Cora, in part playing but in part telling her to clean up the mess.

Cora looked at me, upset: "Crystal did NOT do that!"

"Really? Are you sure?" I knew I hadn't done it.

"I did that!" she said.

Again, "Oh." This was the first of many stereotypes I held about these see-through companions to break. Undoubtedly some children blame their invisible friends when cornered by a parent, but scapegoating is not necessarily the reason they exist, any more than falsely blaming a sibling exhausts one's relationship to a sister or brother. Under attack, children (like adults) are tempted to point elsewhere. But the incident made me wonder. If not compensation for a lack of visible friends, if not someone to blame, why do children have invisible friends? For that matter, why do they pretend anything at all? A stuffed animal becomes a pet, plastic becomes Ninja Turtles, or sand turns into a castle on Mars where superheroes live. What is going on in the psyche of a child that dreams up faithful friends nobody sees and transfigures the visible world into fantasy?

A few weeks after meeting Crystal, I went to our public library in Osh-kosh and happened upon a video of an old Jimmy Stewart movie I'd heard about but had never watched. *Harvey* was originally a Broadway play written by Mary Chase and was made into a movie in 1950. Stewart plays Elwood P. Dowd, a likeable sort who spends a good portion of his time in the local bar befriending all and introducing them to his friend Harvey, a six-foot, three-and-a-half-inch rabbit seen only by Elwood. As if to explain Harvey, Elwood says he's a *púca*, a shapeshifting fairy of Celtic legend. Everyone thinks Elwood has lost his mind and eventually his family tries to commit him to an asylum. Elwood tells the doctor, "Well, I've wrestled with reality for thirty-five years, Doctor, and I'm happy to state I finally won out over it."

When you're watching the film, it is difficult not to side with El-wood—he is so considerate with people, open to whatever comes, and the kind of person you would want to, well, hang out with in a bar. It is as if his openness to Harvey has opened him to the good in others and in life itself. "Years ago my mother used to say to me, she'd say, 'In this world, Elwood, you must be,'—she always called me Elwood—'In this world, you must be oh so smart, or oh so pleasant.' Well, for years I was smart. I recommend pleasant. You may quote me.'"

When his family realizes that the medical treatment of the asylum will likely take Harvey away from Elwood, they decide they'd rather have the pleasant Elwood with an invisible rabbit than take the chance that Elwood would become, as the taxi driver puts it, "a perfectly normal human being—and you know what stinkers they are."

Between Harvey and Crystal and a little girl who would not allow her friend to be falsely accused, my curiosity went into gear, but I had no idea what to do about it. Within a couple of years, Crystal disappeared, and my interest in the subject went dormant. And then it returned. I blame Mexico.

Cora had just started college and Jane and I went to the Yucatán to work on our Spanish. The first weekend, we took a bus from the coast to the small town of Valladolid in order visit the ancient Mayan ruins of Chichén Itzá nearby. On the ride, a movie played: *Millions*, a Danny Boyle story set in England about a Catholic schoolboy, Damian, who finds lots of money along the railroad tracks. Damian is frequently visited by saints of the Church—Claire and Francis of Assisi, for starters—as well as by his own mother, who had recently died and who may also be a saint. These figures, invisible to others, guide him to be generous and give the money to the poor.

Later in the day, as we hiked around the magnificent temples, statues, and columns of the ancient city, I was flooded with images of Mayan deities and spirits, which swirled in my imagination with Francis and

Damian and a little girl's long-lost imaginary friend. The next morning when I awoke, I scribbled these words in my journal: "Booknotes—IF (Imaginary Friends)." I knew it was time. I remarked in the journal how the trip reawakened the dream of exploring imaginary friends more fully. After winding down the project I was working on at the time, a book called *Original Knowing* (OK), I would start working on the subject of IFs. That was ten years ago now, but in my mind's eye, as I put down my pen and close the journal, I can almost see a white rabbit running by.

Returning from Mexico, I began to read everything I could get my hands on about imaginary friends, which turned out not to be that much. A literature review reveals that interest in the topic has been around for over a hundred years, but it has been sporadic at best and largely limited to articles in psychological or educational journals. The earliest study I could find on the subject was published in 1895 by Stanford education professor Clara Vostrovsky who collected examples of imaginary companions from several teenagers and adults remembering back to childhood. She opens the article with a lyrical description of a little girl of ten watching the shadows cast at night by the lamp on the table: "In this shadow-land lives a family, of five members like her own. But they are very different from her relatives. They are shadowy and indistinct and mysterious to her and through some association of ideas, she calls them the Looking glasses."

The earliest book I could find on the subject was written by a professor of psychology at a school for teachers, *Imaginary Playmates and Other Mental Phenomena of Children*, published in 1918. And what a delight the author's last name is: Harvey! It makes me wonder whether Mary Chase had read the book (I have found no evidence one way or the other). Nathan Harvey believed that psychology for teachers concerned itself too much with what children had in common and neglected all the individual differences teachers inevitably encounter in a classroom. Some children see number forms, hear or feel colors, or invent languages, and some children, Harvey writes, "have playmates that are wholly imaginary, but which are as vivid and real to them as living playmates would be." Harvey believes teachers would do well to better understand the minds of such children.

By far the best book I read came eighty-one years later, by developmental psychologist Marjorie Taylor. Whereas the earlier studies had collected stories from teens and adults who were looking back, Taylor had interviewed children themselves. Her 1999 *Imaginary Companions and the Children Who Create Them* is a first-class social-scientific study of childhood imaginary relationships. I found the descriptions of the imaginary companions themselves often to be the most intriguing aspect of the research, and I wondered whether I too could collect stories from children or parents or other adults remembering back.

But my questions were more than psychological. My training is in religion, I am married to a pastor, and I teach in a theological school that trains ministers and pastoral counselors. My temperament and education have made it impossible for me to avoid questions of meaning generally and especially questions of religious meaning. What are the religious implications of the fact children so easily create relationships with inanimate objects, let alone with completely invisible figures? Could there be a connection between a child's relationship to an invisible friend and humans' relationships to invisible beings—from angels and ancestors to ghosts and gods? The religious atmosphere around the planet is loaded with see-through populations and has been for millennia. Is there something fundamentally human about the religious imagination? Or maybe it's all a mass fantasy as Sigmund Freud argued? Or both? Big questions, too big perhaps. Still, I began to sense that I was stepping through a looking glass where childhood imagination mingles with reflections of the sacred.

In the limited research that had been carried out, the connections to the religious world, to the religious imagination, are cloudy at best. Taylor's book mentions that some Christian children named Jesus as an imaginary companion, but she is clear that these children think of the deity in a different way, as real and not pretend. Even so, I thought, there's got to be some overlap. Harvey, the person, also encountered "spiritualistic" interpretations of invisible friends: the constant companion of a five-year-old girl was her twin sister, who had died at two; a six-year-old boy began seeing his father, who had died when the boy was two. Harvey dismisses any mystical explanation. But again, I wondered.

Over the past decade, the white rabbit of my curiosity has led far away from Oshkosh: to Louisville, Kentucky, where I live now; across the Atlantic to England; to the equator in Kenya; on south to Malawi; to nine and three-quarters times zones away in Nepal; and finally to the Dominican shores on the Caribbean, where Cristal now keeps company with another little girl. The more time I have spent with children and their invisible friends, with their willingness to share and talk with me, with their delight in play, with their imaginations, with their smiles, the more I am impressed and encouraged by these friendships. Like Elwood P. Dowd, something about a heart and mind open to seeing a large white rabbit named Harvey may help disrupt whatever turns us into perfectly normal stinkers. The eye that can see through the perfectly normal surfaces of reality to something more gives this adult hope.

Not long after completing the interviews feeding this book, I was sitting in our favorite local theater with my family watching Pixar's animated movie *Inside Out*. The film features an eleven-year-old girl, Riley, and her personified emotions (Joy, Anger, Sadness, Disgust, and Fear), who sit at the control panel "inside" her, at headquarters. At a critical moment in the story, when Joy and Sadness are wandering around lost in the long-term

memory department of Riley's mind, another character appears, Bing
Bong. He is pink and wears a bow tie, a vest, and an undersized derby
hat. "What exactly are you supposed to be?" Sadness asks him.

"You know it's unclear," he answers. "I'm mostly cotton candy,
but shape-wise, I'm part cat," he says, shaking his fluffy tail. "I'm part
elephant," he says, displaying his long trunk, "and part dolphin," he fin-
ishes, with a dolphin cry. Bing Bong is Riley's long-lost, but not totally
forgotten, imaginary friend.

Cora elbowed me, and we laughed way too loudly.

Bing Bong guides Joy and Sadness through hidden and sometimes
treacherous parts of Riley's mind. At one point, entering the chamber of
Abstract Thought, they almost deconstruct themselves out of existence.
I don't want to spoil the story except to say that, in the end, Bing Bong
helps Joy and Sadness return home.

———————

At times I have wondered what see-through companion has guided
the adventures described here. Certainly many a visible angel hosted,
helped, and encouraged the work of it. Several you'll meet through the
pages before you. But now and then I sense more, despite my ordinary
stinker mind trained in the chambers of abstract thought. A long-lost
friend perhaps? Maybe a tall púca or helpful ancestor, a dream figure or
guardian spirit. "We are lived by powers," W. H. Auden once wrote, "we
pretend to understand." Crystal?

PART I
Home

4

LIFE-GIVERS

*She had peeped into the book her sister was
reading, but it had no pictures or conversations in
it, "and what is the use of a book," thought Alice,
"without pictures or conversation?"*

MEET QUACK-QUACK, a four-year-old imaginary duck. Nathan, who created the drawing, was also four years old when we met. He called Quack-Quack one of his "pretend friends," to distinguish him from the kind I'd be able to see without the help of crayons. And there were more: Tadpole, who was one year old and one inch long; Jump-Jump and Jump-Jax, brothers who were eight; and Daisy, a robin who was one hundred years old and Nathan's favorite, his "best pretend friend." While Nathan is not the boy's real name—new names were made up for all the children discussed here to protect their anonymity—the names of the imaginary friends, paradoxically, are real.

As I walked across the campus where I teach, I wondered whether it had been a mistake suggesting the school as a location for the interview with Nathan. Not only are we a theological training ground, we train marriage and family therapists as well, and I was about to meet Nathan and his father in our counseling center, which clearly says Counseling Center at the entrance. It was otherwise ideal for talking with children since the center not only had a room with toys and stuffed animals, but it also had cameras and a one-way mirror for observation, much as you see on cop shows. A parent could stay on the other side of the mirror while the conversation with the child took place. That was great for preventing a parent from answering for a child, but the more I considered the context, the more I worried that Nathan's dad would think that we think that something is wrong with a child with an imaginary friend, let alone, as it turned out, a boy with several.

Nathan himself was too young to read, at least too young to read the big words of the sign. A bright, outgoing boy, he wore an Indianapolis Colts sweatshirt for the interview and a nearly constant smile. He was delighted to talk about his pretend friends. And despite my concern, I quickly discovered that his father was more than okay with my interviewing Nathan, whatever the context. Dad was actually excited by my interest as he too had befriended imaginary companions as a child. He loved the idea that Nathan could help a project designed to better understand children and their imaginative play. In fact, they had hoped Nathan's older brother, Sam, seven years old at the time, would talk to us as well. He too had several pretend friends. But Sam declined the invitation. According to his parents, Sam was shyer about his friends. Even though imaginary characters were fully accepted into this household, Sam was old enough—and self-conscious enough—to realize that others might not be as hospitable to his imagination as his family. And the more I would dig into this research, the more I would realize the price children pay for cognitive "development." Growth into the adult world comes with suspicion and anxiety for things invisible. I wonder at times what kind of mind is actually developing if invisible characters and friendships have to leave to make room for it, or even if they do manage to hang on for a while, you can't talk about them. In the end, I did find older children who were willing to talk about their imaginary relationships with me, yet they did so with caution, as if there were a sign over my head saying Slow: Adults NOT at Play.

You may or may not be surprised to learn that on a few occasions, I had adults approach me: "In your research, have you run across any adults who have imaginary friends?" An academic who can lose herself in imaginary adventures with her friend; an artist who finds continued inspiration from her childhood invisible horse; a pastor who found a healing presence in the form of a wise elder woman from his home country; and a therapist who regularly interacts with dream figures in what Carl Jung called active imagination. In these instances I was surprised by the eagerness of these high-functioning citizens of the adult world to share their stories with me. Mine was certainly research focused upon children and childhood imagination, but it was as if these adults were wanting to stay connected to something or someone, to a friendship that still held meaning and power. Something as simple as my interest in invisible friends made me a friend, an ally, to their own imaginations.

Even so, I discovered after the interview with Nathan that he too, as open as he was, had held back. Talking with his father, I commented upon all the wonderful pictures his son had drawn of these five different friends. His father responded, "Well, on the way to our interview, Nathan told me he actually has five more friends, but he wasn't going to talk about them. When I asked him why not, Nathan said, 'They told me not too.'"

Nathan was one of forty children between two and nine years old that our research team interviewed over the course of a year, children recruited from local schools and churches where I live in Louisville, Kentucky. Nathan's menagerie of friends challenged two assumptions I had held before arranging any interviews. One assumption was that a child would only have one imaginary friend, perhaps a kind of alter ego, but singular nonetheless. After all, Cora had only Crystal. "He has several friends," Nathan's mother said to me as we were setting up a time, "but I'll let him tell you about them." The second assumption was that imaginary friends would be more or less human. His mother hadn't mentioned their animal nature. When I asked his father, privately, about all the animals, he explained that Nathan's pretend friends had once been human, but about the time he started going to preschool, they became animals. "Maybe it's because he has lots of kid friends now?" his father wondered aloud. I soon discovered that Nathan was not alone in having multiple nonhuman friends.

Andrea was four at the time of the interview and had been playing with her imaginary friends for about a year, according to her mother, beginning with Biah-Biah—a girl who was sometimes an M&M with arms and legs. Perhaps she drew the idea from the television commercials featuring animated versions of the candy. But, like Nathan, she had multiple "imagination friends," as she called them, some candyish, some human and otherwise. There was a girl, Lacey, who wore old-fashioned skirts, and Han, who had no eyes and got in trouble a lot. Her friend Eliana, according to Andrea, was under her sleeve during the interview, while Hein was under the carpet. In addition, there was Teapot ("I call her Tea," Andrea explained), "who was a boy and is now a girl—she changes." Her mother thought Andrea got the idea for Tea from the animated film *Beauty and the Beast*, which featured a singing teapot, Mrs. Potts. Though Andrea had based two of her imagination friends upon characters anyone could see on film or television, nonetheless she pointed out that "you can't really see them." In addition, she provided another drawing of Han at the end of the interview because, she explained, he looked different from when she drew him the first time, the day before.

Biah-Biah

Tea

For some children, naming their friends is not a priority. Three-year-old Eva liked to play with her "babies," as she called them, often having tea parties with them. "She loves to serve tea to each of them," her mother explained. She went on to tell how Eva, "right before Christmas, went through a period of setting up a chair, like a teacher, and reading to all of her friends." It may be no accident that her mother is a teacher, a professor at a nearby college, and books and reading fill their home. Eva's mother also had imaginary friends as a child, but for her the names were more important—and memorable. She listed them as she counted on each finger: "Eenie, Meenie, Miney, Punny, and Potsah." She laughed a little as the names came to her so easily, some three decades later.

I thought of Lucy, a kind woman of seventy-something in our church who sits right behind me. A couple Sundays earlier she told me, "Jane told me about your research, and I'm so excited. I told her I've got to

Han

tell Brad about my imaginary friends." Her eyes beamed as if she were a child again. "I had *meetings* with them!" Presbyterians are organization-ally notorious for the number of committees and meetings we have, and we both chuckled at the idea of her young self playing to stereotype.

"How many imaginary friends were there" I asked, "that you had to have meetings?"

"I'm not sure, but there was a room full of them. And," she smiled, "I used to take minutes!" She hoped she could find them for me.

So how does one go about finding children with imaginary friends to inter-view? The short answer: Slowly, with a lot of help. And a cute logo doesn't hurt. This icon with its call for invisible friends topped a flyer posted all over town in shop windows and on church bulletin boards. Electronic versions were sent to pastors, principals, and organizations working with children and parents. Of course, by putting the question mark in the icon, we were not only asking, "Does your child have an invisible friend?" but we were also playing with the letters *IF*, which function both as an acro-nym (as in my journal in Mexico) and as a kind of question or possibility, as in "What if?" Or "What if they are real?"

The flyer was directed to parents of children who have invisible friends. The body explained the project, who I am, and importantly, that the project conformed to the ethical standards of research with human subjects, ensuring that those involved would not be manipu-lated, stressed, or mistreated in any way and that their identities would be disguised to guarantee anonymity. Anyone still con-cerned could contact my dean. Interested parents were instructed to call me, and when they did,

Calling All Invisible Friends!

IF Project Logo

I answered any questions they had, and if they felt good about the project, we scheduled an interview with the child. I also suggested that they ask their children to draw a picture of the friend. Some did, and this proved to be a great conversation starter with a child. "Oh, is this Quack-Quack? Tell me about your friend." Other children drew pictures during the interview.

Recruiting through parents is not the only way to study imaginary companions. Some researchers start with children. They face challenges either way. The challenge of asking parents is that some may not know, or may not want to admit, that their child has an imaginary friend. The challenge of asking children is that they too may not want to admit the friend to relative strangers. Or the opposite could be true. Children may invent one to please these adults. As Marjorie Taylor points out, a child might think, "A pretend friend? What a good idea!" I can't be sure but I may have witnessed such an instance of this spontaneous friend creation while visiting our niece and her family.

"Do any of you have imaginary friends?" Jane asked our great-nephews after explaining my research.

"Oh yeah," one of them, eight years old, answered to the collective surprise of his four brothers and mother, and he went on to describe this figure he often played with.

Later, out of earshot of the boys, his mother said, "He just made that up."

It could be that her son had simply never mentioned the imaginary companion before, or it could be that he "just made that up." Even so, the possibility of making up a friend on the spot suggests the imagination does not easily conform to the best-laid plans and parameters of a research protocol. Again to quote Taylor: "When it comes to imaginary companions, variability is the name of the game."

If a study is trying to determine the prevalence of children with imaginary friends, who is asked can make a difference, adding to the variability. Historically, estimates of how many children have them are all over the place, from Nathan Harvey's 6 percent to as high as 65 percent by Yale psychologists Dorothy and Jerome Singer. Harvey relied upon adults remembering back to childhood, a wonderful exercise for hearing stories but not as precise for calculating numbers. The Singers interviewed both children and their parents. Illustrating the variability, 55 percent of parents claimed their children had imaginary playmates, but 65 percent of the kids claimed them. Asking whether a child has ever *had* one versus currently *has* one makes a difference, as does the age of the child (older children have had more time to have had one).

I would later take up this prevalence issue—comparing the numbers of children with imaginary companions across cultures (for more about the variety among the major studies, see the Appendix). But at this point in the research, I was more interested in the stories of imaginary friends than in percentages, so I decided to start with parents. They may have stories about themselves as well as reports about their children. There was no financial reward for participating in the study (except stickers for the child); we assumed a parent would not make up a friend for their child. If for some reason the child did not admit to having the friend to us, say from shyness, then we would stop the interview, give the child a sticker, and say thank you. Even so, nothing was simple.

"My daughter has several stuffed animals that she plays with a lot," the father said on the phone. "But is that what you're looking for?" This dad raised another issue that had to be addressed, one that also affects percentages: what qualifies as an invisible friend? The wording in our recruitment flyer was intentionally open, moving back and forth between the terms *invisible* and *imaginary*: "If you are a parent with a child (3–7 years old) who currently has an imaginary companion (either invisible or, in some cases, based upon a toy or stuffed animal—as in the Calvin and Hobbes comics), we would appreciate a chance to talk with you, and possibly, with your permission, to talk with your child." In the Bill Watterson comic, *Calvin and Hobbes*, which ran in papers across the country from 1985 to 1995, Calvin is a six-year-old boy who has a stuffed tiger named Hobbes who is pictured as just that when adults are around—as a small, cuddly toy. But when Calvin is alone with the toy, Hobbes becomes a giant friend accompanying him on all kinds of adventures.

A similar transformation happens with a certain bear in A. A. Milne's story of Christopher Robin, the name of Milne's son. "Here is Edward Bear, coming downstairs now, bump, bump, bump, on the back of his head, behind Christopher Robin." These words open the story. "It is, as far as he knows, the only way of coming downstairs, but sometimes he feels that there really is another way, if only he could stop bumping for a moment and think of it. And then he feels that perhaps there isn't. Anyhow, here he is at the bottom, and ready to be introduced to you. Winnie-the-Pooh." That toy bear, along with Kanga, Eeyore, Piglet, and Tigger can now be seen in the Children's Center of the New York Public Library. Although their bigger-than-toy personalities and their widely loved adventures are from the imagination of the adult Milne, the original inspiration derived from the relationship between a boy and a plush toy bear.

Given Pooh and Hobbes and a variable imagination that can animate otherwise inanimate objects into subjects, researchers have to determine what constitutes an imaginary friend, at least for the purposes of their studies. And most studies indeed count a toy or stuffed animal if the child seems to endow it with humanlike properties but do not count it when the child simply carries the object around. But this only backs the question up a little further. How does a researcher or parent get inside the invisible mind of a child to determine whether or to what extent the child is endowing stuffed animals with humanlike or Hobbes-like properties? As researchers, we decided we would have to play this by ear and use our best judgment based upon the description parents provide.

When the father of the girl with several stuffed animals asked, "Is that what you're looking for?" I asked him to describe the play. He said, "Well, she just talks and talks with them while they're playing house or school, for example."

I asked, "Do they seem to talk back?"

He paused, thought about it: "No, I think it's a one-way conversation." Together, we decided that these were not quite what we were looking for.

We may have missed some interesting stories, but when I reported the conversation to our research team, we decided that "Do they talk back?" was a good enough question. We had to use it a few more times, and only once did we get an affirmative answer. When I asked the father of a three-year-old girl, Debbie, he replied, "Oh yes! They talk to her all the time and to each other, and Debbie tells us what they're saying." He went on to describe a "dream team" of characters she plays with, whom I later met when I interviewed her. Bear-bo, Be-bo, and I, along with Savannah and Brook-lee, had a lovely conversation as their animator crouched behind a sofa pillow and held them out for me to meet. She spoke words for them much as a puppeteer brings characters to life. Debbie's dream team represents the only interview we conducted in Louisville with imaginary friends based upon objects alone—in this case, stuffed animals.

But interviews with other children demonstrate that drawing strict lines between pretend figures and characters from everyday life is not so easy. Like Andrea's friend Tea above, some children based their pretend friends upon movie characters. Sasha was the oldest child we interviewed in Louisville, a nine-year-old girl who had four companions, all of whom were based upon the *X-Men* movies: "James Logan" (Wolverine), Scott Summers (Cyclops), Ororo, and Jean Grey. If you know anything about the *X-Men* comics or movies, you know Jean Grey has the special powers of telepathy and telekinesis. Sasha drew Jean Grey and even provided a caption, explaining how she has trouble reading minds, that she was still learning how to use her powers: "I can understand," Sasha said, "because if I could read minds, it would be hard!"

When asked how long she had had these characters as imaginary friends, Sasha said since she was seven, when she first saw the *X-Men* movies. That made us wonder whether these characters with whom she played were really of the same cloth as the pretend friends of other children. We had not planned to interview Sasha; she showed up with her six-year-old sister, Tammy, for whom we had set up the interview. Their grandmother explained that Sasha surprised her with the news that she had pretend friends too, so brought her along. I thought this could be an older-child version of "A pretend friend! What a good idea!"

Jean Grey

They all have powers, hers is:

She can read peoples minds
She has trouble Doing it.

Or, perhaps, she just didn't want to be left out of the action. Yet two comments suggest that Sasha's heroic companions may at least have been in IF territory. First of all, not all *X-Men* characters qualified. For example, "James Logan [Wolverine] has a brother," she explained, "but he's bad, so I don't make him a friend." That is, she exercised discretion concerning which characters were allowed into her world of pretend. Sasha also explained that before the *X-Men* characters, she had made up friends, presumably like other children with imaginary friends (and her younger sister). She said, "When I started making up my own friends, I thought it was weird. But when we started watching *X-Men I* and *X-Men II*, I started getting the idea to use them." Interesting language, I thought: the idea to "use them" as a basis for pretend characters in play so that it would not seem so weird to her. Perhaps this was related to her age and a level of self-consciousness concerned with the opinions of others.

Another child who drew from the visible world to create invisible characters was four-year-old Josie. But hers came with a twist. Her mother was a student at the school where I teach and when she heard about the research, she dropped me an email: "Brad, I just wanted to let you know about Josie's 'friends.' Since we have moved she often plays with 'pretend' Briana. Her best friend where we used to live was Briana and since she can't see her any more she pretends to play with her." But after explaining Briana, Josie's mother went on to describe other friends: "She has a spot behind the sofa where she plays, and she often sits back there and talks to her 'prince.' Then there is 'puppy.' Puppy is her best friend (a stuffed animal) and I often peek in on her having conversations with puppy." She concluded: "She is four years old and has a very, very active imagination!"

We met with Josie and found her open about prince and puppy but a bit hesitant to talk about "pretend Briana." She was very comfortable with the interviewer, Katrina, who was also her neighbor in our school's apartment complex. Katrina asked, "Can you tell me about pretend Briana?" Josie didn't say anything at first, but as Katrina took a moment to decide whether to let it go, Josie offered, "She's, well, a girl who knows she's pretend." Met with a smile from Katrina, Josie's voice picked up as she continued, and her shyness about the friend faded. Josie seemed to want to make sure that we understood that she understood that this was not the "real Briana."

Movies, television commercials, stuffed animals, and friends (the kind anyone can see) all fed these particular imaginations for play and companionship. Yet, many children make up their invisible friends from nothing so obvious or tangible—Quack-Quack and Crystal had no visible counterparts. Rather than drawing hard distinctions between these various forms of play and imagination, I am inclined to think of them all living in close proximity, or as the Singers call it, the same "house of make-believe." Children may borrow a character from another source, but the children themselves write the stories, much as a fan fiction writer borrows from another author. In this way the characters are unlike cultural figures such as Santa Claus or the tooth fairy, who not only come to the child from the outside but are supported (to various degrees) by parents, friends, media, and stories by others.

Hearing about this research, one young man I spoke with wanted to tell me his "imaginary friend story," as he called it. "One day when I was a little kid, I told my mom, 'There's no one to play with.' She told me I should make up an imaginary friend for company. So I tried. I pretended someone was there with me playing with Legos. But," he paused for a moment, "it just didn't work." He explained, "It was boring; he never built anything!" These companions are not easily ordered into being by parents or by willpower. Something deeper, more indirect, animates these relationships.

In his memoir, *Memories, Dreams, and Reflections*, Carl Jung writes that "there are things in the psyche which I do not produce, but which produce themselves and have their own life," an insight he says he gained from a figure in his imagination, Philemon. Jung, as an adult, engaged in regular conversations with imaginary figures who appeared in his night and day dreams. It began with Elijah, a wise old man with a white beard, with whom he held long conversations, which, Jung points out, "I did not understand." Elijah eventually became Philemon, a kind of inner guru who would accompany him on walks and at times "seemed to me quite real, as if he were a living personality. I went walking up and down the garden with him." Jung says that Philemon challenged his assumptions about the world of thought and imagination. "He said I treated thoughts as if I generated them myself, but in his view thoughts were like animals in the forest, or people in a room, or birds in the air, and added, 'If you should see people in a room, you would not think that you had made those people, or that you were responsible for them.'"

I am neither a Jungian nor an analyst, but I too am challenged and intrigued imagining that wisdom and its emissaries like Philemon originate from a source deeper than our own heads. Over the years, I have heard fiction writers speak similarly of their characters. They appear in the imagination and take on a measure of autonomy. Such a strange space, beyond the full control of the author even as the author makes them visible in the imaginations of readers. Novelist Frederick Buechner speaks of the surprise he felt when one of his characters—a questionable figure called Leo Bebb—turned out to be a saint. "He was fat and as full of bounce as a rubber ball," Buechner recalls. Over time, the writer discovered Bebb was good company, without pretense, and so extraordinarily alive that he says, "I couldn't wait to get to my study every morning. That's when I began not only to see that he was a saint but to see what a saint is." And that is a life-giver. Buechner learned that a saint has the same hang-ups and abysses as everyone else. "But if a saint touches your life, you come alive in a new way."

As I look back on the research now, I realize I may well have been studying saints. These invisible and somewhat questionable figures, from Quack-Quack and Tadpole to Crystal and Tea, making themselves known to children and eventually to me. Life-givers. Or maybe the saints were the children themselves, who opened their hearts to share them. Or both.

FLEXIBILITY

*The rabbit-hole went straight on like a tunnel for
some way, and then dipped suddenly down, so
suddenly that Alice had not a moment to think
about stopping herself before she found herself
falling down a very deep well.*

"I'M GOING TO ASK YOU some questions about friends, okay?"
Katrina, a member of our research team, was interviewing four-year-
old Amy, who was happy to talk about her friends. "Now some of your
friends are like the kids on your street or at school, the ones you play
with. Do you have a good friend from school or home you play with?"
Amy named her friend Elly. "Now some friends," Katrina explained, "are
different, maybe ones that other people can't see. Do you have a friend
like that?" Amy did: Cinderella.

Katrina invited Amy to draw a picture of Cinderella. Obliging,
she proceeded to draw her with a white crayon on white paper. A see-
through Cinderella. When she realized that we would not be able to see
her drawing very well she switched to a bolder purple.

Clearly the name Cinderella was borrowed from the story, but, Amy
explained, she was a "little girl" rather than the princess. Earlier in the
week however, according to Mom, Cinderella had been a blue dog.

About six months after the interview with Amy, I had a follow-up
note from her mother, announcing that "Cinderella has left the building."

Cinderella

She went on to explain that her daughter "graduated from pre-K on Tuesday and after coming home announced that Cinderella was gone now that she had graduated." Cinderella, her daughter said, had "gone to the beach" and would not be going to kindergarten. Her mother ended the note saying, "I will miss Cinderella."

I didn't think to ask whether beach-going Cinderella was a little girl or blue dog or something altogether new.

I soon discovered other children who have a friend that takes on multiple forms. Tammy is the younger sister of Sasha (who played with *X-Men* characters). Tammy, six years old at the time of the interview, described her two IFs, Bob and Jeff, contrasting them with her "real friends." Tammy explained that she met Bob and Jeff "at Chucky Cheese on my sixth birthday." Bob was "a five-year-old boy who is really good at karate," and "he can do lots of tricks on the monkey bars." Jeff was a little older, at seven, and "sometimes is a girl, Jeffette, who likes to wear diamond jewelry."

Another flexible friend comes from Kent, who was one day short of eight years old when we talked with him. Kent's friend is Dino, pronounced with a long *i* sound, as if short for dinosaur. On this day Dino was a dragon, with lots of scales, and could hurl thunderbolts and fireballs. "But," Kent explained, "he is always changing." Kent's mother said that he had always had imaginary friends, since he began talking. "I never quite know who's who," she said. But Dino seems to have been around the longest, evolving, becoming more complex as Kent grew older. Though Kent's household had no religious affiliation, his mother explained that Kent's older sister (eleven at the time) had her "angels," invisible companions who hung out with her until she was around nine

Bob

Jeff / Jeffette

years old. As far as Mom knew, the angels didn't change like Dino, who was typically an animal of one sort or another. Except when he was a space alien. Kent's mother said that she had not had imaginary friends, "but when I told my mother [Kent's grandmother] I was doing this, she said she'd had imaginary friends when she was younger."

Dino

Dino, Jeffette, Cinderella. I was not far into the research before I found my own mind needed limbering to accommodate these friends. The everyday adult notion of set forms—you are one gender or the other, you are one species or another, you are from one planet or another— does not necessarily apply to the characters residing in this world of possibilities. In the imagination, something is one thing *and* something else. Categories are flexible. They can be stretched as easily as children touch their toes, transformed as effortlessly as a magician turns silk scarves into doves.

"What are your friends' names again?" Katrina asked, unclear.

"Hee-tome and Boo-gong," four-year-old David answered. "They go to school and work."

Later, David's mother confessed she was as puzzled over the names as anyone, especially since he had other imaginary friends with names a little less curious—Coco, Deepery, and Penguiny. These he called his "kids," two of whom were also stuffed animals. But he made a point of differentiating Hee-tome and Boo-gong as his "friends," who were "super strong" and had been around longer than any of the "kids." One was a red dog, the other a blue dog, and they were always named together. "Hee-tome and Boo-gong celebrate Halloween and Hanukkah," David offered. His mother explained that they were Catholic but that David was attending a Jewish preschool.

When invited to draw a picture of his friends, he first drew three rather formless scribbles on a page. "The red one is Hee-tome," he explained. The next was Boo-gong, made with brown and blue. And the third, all brown, was "their puppy"—that is, the puppy of Hee-tome and Boo-gong. Supplementing this trio of drawings, David decided to draw another picture of his favorite two. Carefully, line by line, he made a colorful grid and explained that these "are the legs of Hee-tome and Boo-gong." More specifically, the yellow lines "are the legs," the pink and red ones "their muscles" and the blue lines are "the jumping/ go up muscles."

David's friends and kids were not so much of the flexible variety as we had found among some children, but his sense of space and time were. Hee-tome and Boo-gong were "getting old" according to David, 909-70 years (spoken as "nine hundred nine-seventy"). They normally lived behind the family on "Wally Paper Street," but at that moment his friends were in Florida, at Salmon Lake, a vacation spot for the family. They were returning soon, "on an airplane." In fact, during the interview David told us that Hee-tome and Boo-gong were traveling at that moment, going "from Florida to the Bahamas, then to Mexican [sic]." Though they normally traveled by air, sometimes they would just appear. For example, at the beginning of our conversation, Hee-tome and Boo-gong were at Salmon Lake, then on an airplane, and suddenly, while David was drawing their picture, the pair joined us. "They're under the table now."

I reported the amazing travel abilities of Hee-tome and Boo-gong to my daughter, who was in college at this time. Cora said, "A tesseract!" She was referring to one of her favorite books growing up, *A Wrinkle in Time*, by Madeleine L'Engle. The novel has been treasured not only by her but by at least a couple of generations of children since it was first published in 1963, as the world continues to grapple with the implications of Einstein's theories of relativity. The main characters, Meg, Charles Wallace, and Calvin, with the help of three other-than-human friends, are able to travel to distant worlds in an instant. Mrs. Whatsit, Mrs. Who, and Mrs. Which are able to wrinkle the fabric of space-time with a *tesseract*, a concept more recently invoked in the film *Interstellar*. The novel diagrams the idea by showing two hands

OPPOSITE *Legs of Hee-tome and Boo-gong*

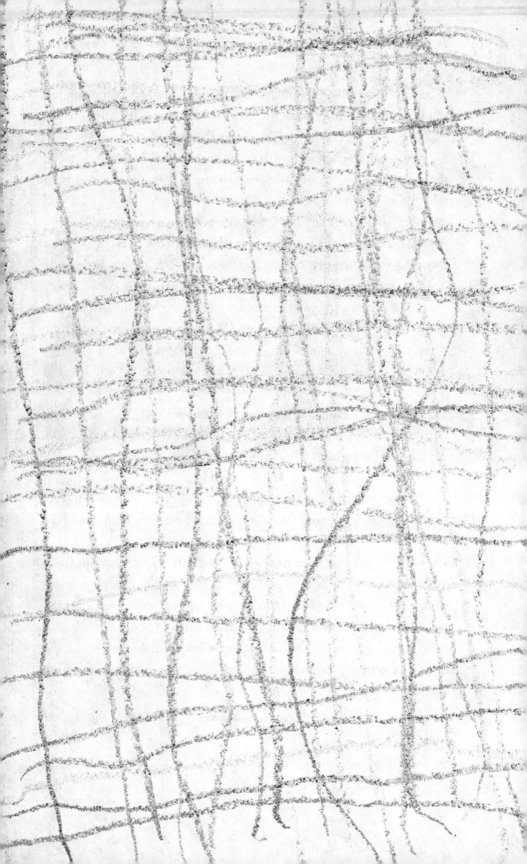

holding a piece of string taught. On the string an ant is crawling off
the left hand about to make the long journey across the string to the
right hand. The next illustration shows the hands held together, with
the string looping below, like so much space-time. The ant is now on
the right hand. Apparently, as Cora suggested, Hee-tome and Boo-gong
have mastered the tesseract.

A few days later I picked up the book and began rereading. I thought
back over some of our interviews, especially when I came to a section
revealing the true identity of Mrs. Whatsit. "Her plump little body
began to shimmer, to quiver, to shift." Mrs. Whatsit transforms before
the children's eyes into a beautiful creature. "She was a marble white
body with powerful flanks, something like a horse but at the same time
completely unlike a horse." She has the head, torso, and arms of a man
now, and to complete the picture: "From the shoulders slowly a pair of
wings unfolded, wings made of rainbows, of light upon water, of poetry."
L'Engle's cosmos is indeed filled with flexibility.

But when the book reveals the age of Mrs. Whatsit, I thought specifically of Hee-tome and Boo-gong.

"'Just how old *are* you?' Calvin asked her."

"'Exactly 2,379,152,497 years, 8 months, and 3 days. That is according to your calendar, of course, which even you know isn't very
accurate.'"

Mrs. Whatsit, despite her two plus billion years, turns out to be
the youngest of the three Mrs. Ws. And the notion of 909-70 didn't
seem quite as odd anymore. More importantly, I began to see better the
connection between imaginative literature such as *Wrinkle* and childhood thinking in general. Is this part of the appeal? In fantasy reading
or science fiction, time and space are not what they seem to be, they are
malleable and full of inexhaustible possibilities.

David's parents had made an intriguing discovery the night before our interview, one illustrating again looser conceptions of space and time. Many parents reported more extended conversations with their children about invisible friends before an interview, sometimes as the child drew pictures, or sometimes while explaining the child would be meeting someone who wants to hear more about Quack-Quack or Hee-tome and Boo-gong. In the case of David, over dinner the night before, he informed his mother and father that Hee-tome and Boo-gong not only play with him, but that they were friends with Jo-Jo. And who is Jo-Jo? Jo-Jo was the imaginary friend of David's father when he had been a child. David's invisible friends and Dad's invisible friend were friends.

Jo-Jo, by the way, was 99.

Listening to David, I thought about the first paper I wrote for my PhD program, over two decades earlier, about the world-renowned Swiss psychologist Jean Piaget. Nobody has had more influence upon Western thinking about child development since Freud, and understanding Piaget's work was crucial to my own. While Freud rarely worked directly with children, Piaget did, employing all variety of simple props—modeling clay, bottles of liquid, dolls—to test the ways in which children think.

My paper was specifically about Piaget's research into children's understanding of time. The world had just delayed the turn from 1987 to 1988 by one second, adding a second to the year, and it made me time-curious. Piaget had said that his research was inspired "by a number of questions kindly suggested by Albert Einstein." No surprise to parents that for young children the meaning of a "day" or "week" is vague, at best. A three-year-old may refer to something that happened weeks before as "yesterday" or a birthday party she knows is coming as "tomorrow." A four-year-old may say that Dad is older than Granddad because Dad is taller. So, if babies do not emerge from the womb able to read a clock, how do children learn time? What mental tool or ability must develop? Logic. The answer for Piaget is always *logic*. The capacity for understanding the relations between objects, cause and effect, necessary sequences, and mathematical order is what marks the mature mind, including understanding time. Piaget characterized the developmental period from two to seven years as "preoperational," by which he meant prelogical, a period of *magical thinking*. Later, children transition to "concrete operations"; they can work logically in some ways, as long as there are concrete objects involved (ten marbles take away three marbles leaves seven). With puberty comes "formal operations." Children can engage in abstract thought which opens the door to formal logic (Socrates is human; all humans are mortal; therefore Socrates is mortal).

In the case of time, the most fundamental issue, as Piaget describes it, is the ability to understand sequences, or how one thing happens before another, a form of logic. He tested children by showing them a series of events: for example, pouring liquid from one bottle to another. Then he would ask the children to retrace the sequence. Even with pictures to remind them of the various steps, young children were poor at the task. That is, even five-year-olds had trouble reconstructing simple sequences.

Magical thinking + time = 909-70 years.

I turned the paper in with fear and trembling. Not only is Piaget difficult to read, but my professor had worked with him during a sabbatical in Switzerland. Dr. Loder returned the paper, generally affirmed the effort and thought I got Piaget right. But in the margins, he wondered how work inspired by Einstein's relativity of time and space ended up demonstrating the mental development of classical notions of absolute time and space, notions upset by relativity theory? Like some kind of Zen riddle, he was using logic to challenge logic. After all, aren't tesseracts and a flexible universe closer to Einstein's picture of the universe? Like most professors, he ended with "a good start but it needs more work." It made me curiouser and curiouser, but less about time than about young minds, and it is likely related to why I was listening to children like David describe their flexible friends.

Not long into the research, another pattern emerged among some children, one in which the flexibility of the imaginative mind stretched categories that are otherwise more set. That is the category of life itself—and with it, death.

Deen and Elisabeth were the imaginary friends of Sally, nearly eight years old when we spoke with her. According to Sally's mother, Deen and Elisabeth had been around since Sally was two and a half and "pretty constant," not temporary figures or transitional attachments in the way a stuffed animal often is. "Elisabeth and Deen are almost eight," according to Sally, and had come back with the family from a vacation. Sally said, "They live in an imaginary world." Even so, they were present during the interview. They visited Sally often, "to play games like tag or hide and seek." I found myself wondering whether hiding is easier or harder when you are invisible and imaginary!

Except for the length of time Deen and Elisabeth had been around, her descriptions were not remarkable, relatively speaking. They maintain a stable form, come around during play, and are more or less human. But another figure showed up occasionally to be with Sally: Paw-Paw John, her grandfather. Paw-Paw John died when Sally was still a baby, so she had no living memory of him. But when Sally got sad, "he visits me from heaven and makes me feel better." So tender—this grandfather showing up, as the best grandparents do, with comfort and love.

Aside from the beauty of the description, I realized it created another challenge with terminology. To call Paw-Paw John an *imaginary* companion or friend does not quite do justice to the quality and background of this figure, based as it is on someone who once did live and was visible. Neither Sally nor her parents called him imaginary, even if

her parents—practicing Presbyterians—did not know exactly what to make of these compassionate visits.

Three weeks into interviewing, we met Pauline, who was four years old when we talked with her about her friends: Flower Barbie, Jackson, Stella, and a new friend, Trevor, who happened to appear the day of the interview.

Pauline shared how she played with these friends, but added that Stella was now in heaven. Tragically, there had been a recent and unexpected death of an aunt, through a bicycling accident. Soon afterwards, Pauline declared that "Stella is in heaven with Aunt Isabel." And though

Flower Barbie

death is no easy concept to understand for a child, Pauline understood that her aunt would no longer be present in her life, would no longer be seen or heard.

Reflecting upon Pauline and the loss of her aunt, I am impressed by the way this four-year-old child incorporated the idea of death into her imaginative world. Or perhaps it is more accurate to say that her imagination incorporated death into itself, thereby threading the tragedy into Pauline's life. Stella, her imaginary friend, keeps company with Aunt Isabel, and in a way, keeps a meaningful relationship, and its loss, alive.

Listening again to Pauline's interview, I was reminded of an interview with a little girl conducted not by us but by Harvard psychiatrist Robert Coles for his magnificent book, *The Spiritual Life of Children*.

Natalie was eight years old at the time, a Hopi girl living in New Mexico. She was originally interviewed for one of the volumes of Coles's Pulitzer Prize–winning Children of Crisis series. The series is based upon his conversations with hundreds of children through the 1960s and 1970s, children under the stress of poverty, illness, displacement, and/or racism. Natalie's grandmother was very sick and Natalie knew she was dying. Looking to the mesa in the distance, the girl says to Coles, "She is sick. She is between here and there [the mesa]. She will leave us for there, and then she'll prepare for us to come there." Natalie explained that when we die, we become birds. And for this young soul, the mesa was heaven, where her grandmother would soon fly to join their ancestors. "I woke up yesterday, and I realized I'd been there myself [in a dream] to visit her." Later that day, Natalie overheard her grandmother talking with *her* grandmother.

Coles tells of child after child who draws upon the stories and beliefs of their communities to feed the imagination in the face of life's challenges, especially death. In this case, a little girl finds connection with her ancestors as well as their land through an imagination that easily sees humans transforming into birds and knows a mesa as heaven itself. The connection, like the ones with Paw-Paw and Aunt Isabel, abides through life and death and testifies to the power of relationships and the imagination that supports them.

But this is my bias, an appreciation for the possibilities pregnant in the imagination and religion alike. There are of course other views. In fact, Coles himself, trained in Freudian psychoanalysis, confesses at the beginning of *The Spiritual Life of Children* that he had to struggle with his suspicion of religion he was educated into. Freud famously viewed religion as an *illusion* born of the desire for an almighty father who can protect us from the harshness of life. But the time has come, according to the father of psychoanalysis, to shed such infantilism for "the rational operation of the intellect." No wonder Coles struggled to appreciate the religious beliefs and practices he encountered among children.

While Freud's critique of religion is well-known and oft repeated, less understood is how tied his analysis of religion is to the imagination itself. The heart of what he labels "infantilism" is imagination. Freud understood early childhood to be awash in fantasy, generated by the pleasure principle of the psyche's id to compensate for unmet needs and frustrated desires. When a baby is hungry but not fed, the id throws out a vision of milk to satisfy the stomach. Key here is the belief that young children cannot differentiate fantasy from reality. When you or I have a daydream or an imaginative reverie, we realize soon enough that our mind was somewhere else, not oriented to the reality in front of our eyes. But according to Freud, young children do not know the difference. Milk or a vision of milk—it's the same. All the world's a daydream. So, the journey of child development, in this view, is about becoming more and more reality oriented, which is to say, more and more rational.

Like Coles, I too found myself struggling with this tradition as I listened to children. In my case, the struggle was less directly about Freud and more about Piaget, whose theories I had continued to study and teach all these years since graduate school. What I had not fully realized before I took on this research was the deep influence Freud had upon Piaget. On the surface, they seem very different, with Freud concerned with analyzing the psyche and Piaget focused upon the development of intelligence in children. Yet Piaget was convinced that Freud was right about the young mind, that it is dominated by the irrational and illogical, what Piaget called *ludistic* tendencies, from the Latin for "game" or "play," also the root of *ludicrous*. "The child's mind," he wrote in 1928, "is full of these ludistic tendencies up to the age of 7 or 8, which means that before this age it is extremely difficult for him to distinguish between fabulation and truth."

What I have here been calling flexibility, Piaget calls prelogical fabulation. Development is a process of moving from the foggy magical thinking of id-driven fantasy to the light of scientific, logical, real-world-oriented thought, from the ludicrous to the truth. Imaginative play, in this tradition is a way of compensating for unfulfilled wishes and desires. If a child is not allowed to have a telephone, she compensates for the frustrated desire by turning a wooden block into one. Pretend phone or block, it's all the same to the young mind. So, reading backwards from the phenomenon, a child's imaginary friend must come about through loneliness or the inability to make real friends. The imagination, in this picture, is the great compensator.

Perhaps that is how we should interpret Paw-Paw John, who comes to comfort Sally, and Natalie's dream visit to the ancestral mesa, and Hee-tome and Boo-gong, who suddenly cut through space and time to keep David company. The monarchal id gets what it wants, immediately, compensating for the frustrations of life. As I listened to parents, I could see how deeply such attitudes about the imagination have dug themselves into our cultural mind-set. Many of them reflected a soft version of this compensation assumption as they speculated about the reason their children had imaginary friends: "Well, he's the oldest"; "We recently moved"; "She's an only child"; "He's the youngest child"; "She really likes cartoons"; "He's not allowed to watch television."

Though it was mild, we could detect a whiff of nervousness. There must be some reason my child is making up friends, some lack. And this was among the kind of parents, who almost by definition, were more comfortable with invisible friends than not; otherwise they would not likely have volunteered so readily. The fact that parents don't generally worry in the same way about stuffed animals, dolls, or Ninja Turtles suggests that the anxiety is related to something else—perhaps invisibility. With dolls and stuffed animals, children base personalities and attachments on something concrete, perceivable in the sunlit world, demonstrating that they are not lost in some kind of hallucinated cave of confusion. While the parents I spoke with were not overly worried, I sensed that they worried that maybe they should be worried.

The force of Freud and Piaget is strong. Of course life presents frustrations and unmet desires; of course we get thrown off-center and have to reorient our expectations and thinking to equilibrate; of course children can be egocentric. But is that whole story? I wondered. Only a month into interviewing children, I, like Coles, found myself in a struggle with this tradition. I could feel my own theoretical categories and conceptual tools stretching.

Frankly, it should not have taken a month.

In another situation stretching the boundaries of life and death, a child had an invisible friend who died. The very first interview we conducted for the study was with Nicole, who was only two years and eleven months old, one of the youngest children interviewed. When I first heard about Nicole, from a mutual friend of her mother's, I learned that Nicole had previously had two invisible friends, Leah and Coda, but that one of them, Coda, "had died."

To my surprise, when I met Nicole's mother, she explained that Nicole once again had two imaginary friends. Coda had come back. "Coda died, right Nicole?" Nicole's mother was confirming with her daughter. "But now he's back?" Nicole nodded her affirmation. "How did he die Nicole?" Mother asked.

Nicole looked up at me, then her mother: "He took too big a bite." She offered no further explanation about the death. But we did learn that Leah was older than Coda, and she had white hair and brown eyes. Coda was a bit mischievous at times; for example, he had earlier taken Leah's crown away from her. Was Coda's impish behavior connected to taking too big a bite? I don't know, but perhaps the imaginary friend was helping Nicole play out the world of consequences.

Near the end of our conversation, Jannine, a member of the research team, asked, "Nicole, where are Leah and Coda now?"

Coda and Leah

"Leah's over there," Nicole said as she pointed across the room. We were in a classroom of a preschool, otherwise unoccupied except for us and a couple of invisible friends, give or take.

"And where's Coda?"

Nicole looked around, got up from her chair, and ran across the room to the open door. She stood at the threshold looking up and down the hallway; then she started waving her arm, as if beckoning Coda to come join her. Apparently he did, and Nicole came back into the room. But about halfway to her chair Nicole crouched down in a huddle with her friend. She started talking to him in whispers, her head nodding and hands gesturing in an intense conversation. After all this, Nicole returned to her seat with us and declared, "Now Coda's here too!"

"Oh, that's great," I said to her. I picked up the sheet of stickers. Jannine had already given Nicole a couple. I asked, "Would Leah and Coda like stickers too?"

With that, Nicole looked up at me, stared into my eyes for a moment, and then declared, "They're pretend!" The tone was *They're pretend, silly, don't you know that?* Not even three years old, this tiny child knew the difference between pretend friends and the ones anybody can see, and she was startled when I seemed not to.

Laughing beneath my breath, I started to put the sheet of stickers away. Nicole stopped me, and said cleverly, "But I'll take the stickers for my parents." Of course, I gave them to her.

At the time, I did not immediately think about Freud or Piaget and theories of child development. But I did think, "Kids know the difference between imaginary friends and the visible kind." Something sophisticated was going on in that little almost-three-year-old mind.

I recall reading Freud's *Future of an Illusion* in the first theology course I ever took and having to debate the merits of his arguments. As a class, we had to consider whether the work contained a valid, if not helpful, critique of religion when religion becomes simply a kind of magical belief in a protector or compensator or an other-than-this-world orientation to life. Sure, the class concluded. But I don't remember ever taking up Freud's basic assumptions about the psyche or imagination that gives rise to such an illusion as "God" in the first place.

But I now see more clearly how suspicion of religion and suspicion of imagination are cut from the same Freudian bolt of cloth. We could add myth, animism, fantasy, and imaginary friends as well to the list of suspects, so-called primitive thought to be left behind with our teddy bears for the sake of a hard-boiled realism. Of course, my own view of religion is more generous than Freud's, or I wouldn't be in the business I'm in. I've seen too much life-giving at work through it, all over the world, to be so cynical. (Horrible things happen both in the name of religion and in the name of rationality.) So now I wonder whether we can't be more generous to the world of imagination, adding myth, animism, fantasy, and friends nobody else can see. What if the ability to see invisibles, an awareness of *more*, as William James once put it, is tied to something profound and enduring? What if it speaks to a creative posture in life that sees the world in deeper dimensions?

This is what Robert Coles eventually found in the children he interviewed. His emphasis in *The Spiritual Life of Children* is less about particular religious beliefs and practices—though they are very much included—and more upon children as *soulful*: "young human beings profane as can be one minute, but the next, spiritual." Children confined to iron lungs, children facing racist mobs during desegregation, children trying to make sense of tragedy, all drawing upon their religious traditions, stories, and practices for sustenance, yes, but for more. Coles found them wise.

As Coles walks with Natalie, the young Hopi girl, she is in one moment playing with her dog, Blackie, and the next she is describing a daydream. "I dream of meeting our Hopi ancestors," she says, of a time when all gather together "and the waters of the rivers are full, and the sun has warmed the cold part of the world, and it has given the really hot part a break, and all the people are sitting in a huge circle, and they are brothers and sisters, *everyone*!" Her vision, her reverie, expands. "That's when all the spirits will dance and dance, and the stars will dance, and the sun and the moon will dance, and the birds will swoop down and

they'll dance, and all the people, everywhere, will stand up and dance."
It is a time when fights cease. "No more fights. Fights are a sign that we
have gotten lost, and forgotten our ancestors, and are in the worst trouble.
When the day comes that we're all holding hands in the big circle—no,
not just us Hopis, everyone—then that is what the word *good* means."

Coles hears a strong resonance with biblical prophets in Natalie's
vision of a final roundness of the universe, a dream that stands "in
sharp contrast with the confrontation and opposition that orders most
of human society." The imagination at work here could be, as Freud suggests, the id throwing up fantasies to meet the harshness of a world where
grandmothers are dying, where a people are oppressed by a surrounding
nation. This is possible. Yet Coles sees something more constructive and
hopeful going on: a vision of the good sustaining and guiding a child's
ways of being in the world around her; a vision of the interrelatedness of
the universe shaping her attentive engagement with the birds and land
and ancestors living and dead. For Coles this requires—in psychoanalytic
terms—a robust flexibility of ego.

A flexible imagination that easily allows transformations from one
category to another—whether gender, species, shape, time, space, life, or
death—makes childhood thought a challenge to the adult mind. Yet, as
Coles discovered, maybe that flexibility of spirit is worth our attention.

I was sharing with a friend this remarkable, flexible feature of children's
imaginations. Chris Elwood, historical theologian, asked if I'd read Julian
of Norwich lately. It had been a while. Julian was a fourteenth-century
English mystic, who, in the midst of a life-threatening illness, had a series
of visions, or "showings." "Cataphatic, definitely," Chris said, referring
to the type of mystic she was. "Lots of images."

In theological shorthand, he was reminding me of two basic paths of
mysticism: *cataphatic*, from the Greek for "affirmative," and *apophatic*,

from the Greek for "negative." In the apophatic approach, the emphasis is on negating what we think we know about God, on emptying the mind of images and ideas to make room for union with the God who is beyond the senses and representations. A classic apophatic example, also from the fourteenth century, is *The Cloud of Unknowing* by an anonymous English mystic. Its emphasis is upon clouding or silencing thoughts and images to encounter the Holy. By contrast, the cataphatic approach emphasizes the way in which imagination, memories, and visions open the mystic to knowledge of God. Here, mental images and memories, as well as icons and art, may help us see, or better, see through, to God. "I'll get you a passage," Chris said; he had just assigned it to a class.

In her first vision, Julian is shown a small ball in the palm of her hand and is told that this ball is everything God has made. "It lasts and always will because God loves it; and thus everything has being through the love of God." Definitely cataphatic—an image is seen through to the love of the Creator for everything. But the following is the specific passage Chris was thinking of: "And so I saw that God rejoices that he is our Father, and God rejoices that he is our Mother," writes Julian. I thought of Jeff, who is sometimes Jeffette, and of Tea, who could be a boy or a girl—"and God rejoices that he is our true spouse, and that our soul is his beloved wife." It seems the cataphatic mystical imagination is also limber.

I admit, juxtaposing Tea and Jeffette with visions of God may be a peculiar move, completely illogical and irrational. But I find myself drawn to the intersections all the same. The more I listened to children as they described rich relationships with invisible characters, the more curious I became about the human imagination itself and its way of seeing. I still move cautiously with the connections, but also with a hazy hope that through such crystalline images, we can sense more.

CHAPTER 3

LOGIC AND IMAGINATION

*"Contrariwise," continued Tweedledee, "if it was
so, it might be; and if it were so, it would be; but
as it isn't, it ain't. That's logic."*

"HERE, DO THIS," Leslie said as she handed me a piece of paper and
pencil. On an earlier occasion Leslie, five years old, had told me about
Princess, a pretend friend with whom she played. But, Leslie explained,
she sometimes liked to be Princess and dress like her and wear a crown.
At this moment though, the five-year-old royal had prepared two math
problems for me as if she were the teacher and I her student:

4 + 4 = _____
2 + 6 = _____

I took the pencil, filled in the blanks, and showed her. She said I
got them right.

"Now I've got one for you," I offered, setting down the pencil and
paper.

"What?"

"Just listen to this," I said. "All pigs bark." She looked at me curiously,
but I continued as if we were in school and this were a quiz. "And Porky
is a pig. Okay?" She nodded. "Now, does Porky bark?"

"No, silly," she answered. "Pigs don't bark!" And of course she was right, in one way. But when it comes to this simple reasoning problem, she was as wrong as Piaget would have predicted. It takes a level of abstract thought to disembed the logic from the characters involved. That comes in older childhood, nearer adolescence.

"What if," I posed in a playful voice, "pigs did bark?" She looked at me carefully. "Would Porky bark?"

"Yes," she answered immediately.

"How come?"

"Because Porky's a pig."

My quiz for Leslie was inspired by a series of studies exploring the role of imagination in relation to children's ability to solve syllogisms. Syllogisms are logic problems like the one with which I challenged Leslie. Typically, they present two premises, and a conclusion is deduced from them. A classic from Aristotle:

1) All humans are mortal.
2) Socrates is a human.
3) Therefore, Socrates is mortal.

When posed as a question, the conclusion is to be deduced from the premises: Is Socrates mortal? Yes.

But the logic at work in syllogisms can easily get muddled: all grass is green; vegetables are green: therefore, grass is a vegetable. A silly, if gruesome, illustration comes from the film *Monty Python and the Holy Grail.* A mob has accused an innocent woman of being a witch. A leader in the village, Bedevere, explains that there are ways of determining whether she really is a witch. He works them through a series of Socrates-styled questions to help them deduce the answer: "What do you do with witches?" he asks.

Someone in the crowd answers, "Burn them."

"And what do you burn, apart from witches?"

The answer, "Wood."

"Good. Now, why do witches burn?"

"Because they're made of wood?"

"Good. . . . " This reasoning goes on and on (witches are made of wood, wood floats, as do ducks). Finally, they conclude the best way to determine whether the woman is a witch is by seeing if she weighs the same as a duck.

Ducks and witches aside, developmental psychologists use syllogisms to help identify the point at which we able to demuddle our reasoning and think more clearly about premises and their relationships. Piaget theorized that to do so, we must be able to analyze the *formal* relations between the premises regardless of their empirical reality. Whether or not pigs actually bark doesn't matter and has to be ignored. But a young mind, as Leslie first demonstrated, has difficulty doing so and gets tripped up by the counterfactual premise. So why did she get it right when I posed the question in a playful, what-if mode? Because in the imagination—as we've seen—all kinds of crazy things can happen: incongruities and contradictions, and potentially even pigs barking.

The imagination creates a tesseract, a wrinkle in Piaget's developmental timeline.

The research team of Maria Dias and Paul Harris made the discovery. They posed syllogisms in a way that invited playing along with a make-believe prompt: "Let's pretend that I am in another planet. Everything in the planet is different. I'll tell you what's going on there." The experimenter spoke with play and drama in her voice to communicate they were in a "make-believe mode." "On this planet, all cats bark." . . . The result was that children who were prompted with the make-believe instructions were much more likely to answer the syllogisms correctly (compared to children who were not). Children as young as four were able to solve these tough, counterfactual, incongruent syllogisms correctly. Four! My one-sample study with Leslie found the same. Once placed in the world of imagination, she could play out the logical conclusion.

What a paradox. My no-nonsense, straightforward, serious quiz voice generated the wrong mind-set in Leslie, suppressing her reasoning abilities. The playful what-if, let's-imagine-together voice invited the full powers of her logic to shine on the problem. I came away from the encounter determined to introduce more play and imagination not only in the preschool Sunday school I teach, but in my graduate-level classes as well. Maybe each class should start with some Madeleine L'Engle. Or maybe I could develop a whole class on learning by imagination? Tesseracts 101.

I went back to Harvey—the professor, not the rabbit—and found Ruby C. The encounter with Leslie and Princess, with math problems and barking pigs, reminded me of one of Harvey's descriptions from a century earlier, in the opening chapter of *Imaginary Playmates*. Ruby vividly remembers having two imaginary friends as a child, Katie Fendus and Nellie Brosus. She can still recall how they played—sometimes all together, but at other times Ruby would simply watch the other two play. The part triggering my memory was this: "The three of them sometimes played school, and Ruby remembers that they used to tell her how to spell words." To have imaginary friends who help you with schoolwork is impressive. I thought, "That's learning by imagination!" Yet the story comes with a warning. One word that Katie Fendus and Nellie Brosus taught her how to spell was "meat." They taught her to spell it *m-e-q-f-e-g*, which Ruby points out, in case Harvey had any doubts, "was not correct."

In describing Ruby's friends, I was struck by Harvey's emphasis upon vividness. Katie and Nellie "were as vivid and distinct to her as two living children would be. She could see them very plainly, and could hear the tones of their voices when they were talking." Though it sounds as if Harvey were describing the world of Freudian fantasy, he definitely was not. He had harsh things to say about his contemporary's theory. Fundamentally, it betrayed the principle of parsimony, favoring an overly complex explanation over a simpler approach. Ironically enough, Freud's imagination is to blame, spinning a view of the psyche from the yarn of King Oedipus full of frustrated desires hidden in dreams and fantasies to compensate. I hate to imagine what Freud would make of imaginary friends who can't spell.

Harvey took a very different approach in his "physiological psychology," as he called it. For him, imaginary playmates were simply a by-product of nerve impulses. A particularly energetic nervous system can generate vivid visual and auditory projections—something like the afterimage of an object, a lamp, say, when closing your eyes. In some children, a backflow of energy from the brain to the retina generates images that are "seen as vividly as if they are living children." Neurons firing through the brain can do strange things. Very parsimonious and logical, but I'm not sure Katie or Nellie or Crystal or Jeffette would appreciate being reduced to a retinal image. At least Freud's theory comes with a good story, one firing the imagination with kings and queens, love and murder.

A couple of decades after Harvey, in 1934, Margaret Svendsen published an article about her own research with children who had "invisible characters," as she calls them in the piece. Hers appears to be the earliest study that involves talking with children directly while they are still playing with the characters—that is, not relying upon people remembering back to childhood. Most revealing is the way in which she begins the article. She quotes from sixteen different sources representing various sociological and psychological theories about the phenomenon. They range from the idea that children are compensating for some failure or splitting off some undesirable aspect of themselves to the idea that imaginary friends represent a sign of creativity or intelligence. In her own study of forty children, Svendsen found a great variety of characteristics among the children, from promising leadership skills and "superior intelligence" to "personality difficulties," as she puts it, "with timidity heading the list."

Svendsen concludes the article without resolving the tensions between the various theories, raising instead more questions to be explored. But she set the standard for doing so: talk to kids. On this front, Professor Harvey would likely agree. "Only by a collection of many divergent experiences of different children," he writes, "are we able to comprehend what the actions of any particular child may mean." I found that good advice and it reinforced the resolve to interview more children.

But one thing seemed clear at this point. Between barking pigs and little girls who think I'm silly if I don't understand that Leah and Coda are pretend, imagination and logic are not the sworn enemies of each other that they have been portrayed to be. The idea that development is a process of growing out of magical thinking and into the hard-boiled realism of logical thought cheats the vital relationship between fantasy and reality, between pretend worlds seen in the mind and the sense-based worlds seen with the eyes. What if, I thought, the two are friendly? What if logic and imagination are invisible friends?

One of the stumbling blocks to imagining early childhood as awash in wish-fulfilling fantasy is that children show no signs of pretend play until well into their second or third year. If anything, realism is first, and imagination is the more sophisticated developmental accomplishment, one opening possibilities, even logical ones, in the powers of the human mind.

Decades ago, in what sounds as if it were right out of the worst sort of horror film, Cornell professor Eleanor Gibson invited babies to crawl over a cliff. Or so it seemed. Of course, she never put any children in actual jeopardy. In a study published in *Scientific American* in 1969, Gibson describes a "visual cliff" apparatus her lab created to test whether babies, six to fourteen months old, could perceive depth. A platform with a drop-off was covered with glass. If children did not perceive depth, as assumed, they would crawl right over that drop-off (but not fall since the glass would hold them). Babies were urged by their mothers to crawl towards their loving arms, which would take them over the visual cliff. But the babies did not crawl toward their mommas. They either cried or crawled back in the other direction. Gibson tried the experiment with various animals as well, including two-day-old chicks, and they would not crawl over the cliff either. Realism.

In the decades following that visual cliff experiment, more and more research with babies finds them to be anything but a blank slate or soaked in fantasy. Babies have or rapidly develop definite expectations for the objects and people, the space and creatures around them. They are intuitive physicists and psychologists. By three months, if not earlier, a baby expects a solid object to retain its size and shape and does not expect it to go out of existence when it goes behind another object. They are surprised when experimenters play magic tricks suggesting otherwise. Babies even possess the building blocks of mathematical thinking, an intuitive sense of less and more. They may not be able to count the number of stars on a mobile, but they appreciate the difference between one star and several. Babies also possess an intuitive sense of space. Not only do they perceive depth, but if they are disoriented, they can reorient themselves by the layout, the angles and surfaces of their surroundings.

From birth, babies hunt for and have expectations about the world of people as well. Infants seek out, differentiate, and prefer human faces from other kinds of objects, such as dolls or dummies. They do the same for human speech and movement. They are drawn to mutual eye gazing, and they pick up the emotional life of those around them as well. They grasp the difference between animate and inanimate and expect animated creatures to move under their own power, by their own agency. Also, babies will try to mirror human actions, such as waving, but do not do so for object actions.

In short, these core, intuitive expectations about the world lay the foundation upon which the house of make-believe can later be built.

But what a turnaround. And what a different starting point for considering the imagination and the friends born there. The imagination is not a regressive mode of thought, not inherently inferior or ludicrous. As Alison Gopnik suggests in her book, *The Philosophical Baby*, from an evolutionary point of view, imagination may be one of the most unique and significant aspects of our species. "If our nature is determined by our genes, you would think that we would be the same now as we were in the Pleistocene." But our imaginations bring flexibility and creativity and have allowed our species to travel, adapt to new environments—some very harsh—endure, and thrive. We can pose and try out alternatives to that which is, whether in our individual lives or in the world around us.

The imagination is not simply an annoyance to be tolerated among young children, but it is key to humanity, allowing us to imagine possibilities and improvise our lives.

Paul Harris (one of the syllogism researchers above) has carried out as much research as anyone to tease out the cooperative relationship between logic and imagination, not only with syllogisms but with multiple studies since. He believes that when children engage in imaginative play, they are actually practicing real-world, cause-and-effect, if-then logic. If this happens, then that follows. How did Coda die? "He took too big a bite." Why don't you want to talk about your other pretend friends? "They told me not to." How do Hee-tome and Boo-gong get to Salmon Lake? "They take an airplane."

Children bring what Harris calls "causal maps" with them into the pretend world and work with them. One experiment he conducted with two-year-olds demonstrates how easily children do so. A hand puppet takes an empty carton of milk and pretend-pours pretend-milk in various locations. The children are given a sponge and asked to dry the floor where it's wet. They had no trouble choosing the right locations and "drying" the pretend-wet floor in the right spots. To do so took both imagination and logic. The children easily blend them to play along, to cooperate with the experimenter. In another experiment, toddlers are handed a popsicle stick and asked to show how a teddy bear combs its hair. Without hesitation, they run the stick over Teddy's head in a combing motion. The children are then asked to show how Teddy eats with a spoon; the toddlers put the stick to the bear's mouth and spoon-feed Teddy. Even little two-year-olds possess a flexible imagination that lets a stick be a spoon or a comb, and they possess the if-then logic that knows what to do with the stick given the premise. These may be simple experiments, but they illustrate how easily children bring their if-then thinking into the world of pretend and fantasy and, by doing so, become more adept with the logic that also serves them well in the everyday, nonpretend world.

Instead of muddling about in a fog of primary processes lacking logic or the ability to reason accurately in the real world, nearly from birth children possess a sense-based grasp of their environments and rapidly demonstrate realistic expectations for objects and agents in the world— all before they can speak a word. Such realism does not go away when children learn to pretend; instead it is played with. Children discover they can toy with the softer material of representations and expectations we hold about things like popsicle sticks and combs and spoons, even as everyday logic enters into the play. Pretending takes realism and squares it. Things are what they are, but also something else. The child knows at the level of the sense-based world of seeing and touching that the stick is a stick. But at another level, in the imagination, the stick can be a spoon or comb or a rocket ship or a barking pig. This double knowledge of imagination and logic is at the heart of pretend play.

Logic and imagination are the soul mates of mind, the invisible friends of knowing.

"But what about monsters in the closet?" a student asked. She added, "I had them."

A lot of nods around the room suggested she was not alone. I'd been pointing out how logical young children can be, and I'd shared the Leah and Coda adventures, culminating with the way Nicole straightened me out about her friends ("They're pretend!"). A good question, I thought. If children easily distinguish pretend situations from real-world ones, if they are so logical at even young ages, why do they think monsters are in the closet, or mistake a shadow for a vicious animal? Why do children sometimes confuse their imagination with reality?

"Good question," I said and shared with the class an incident I vividly recall from my own childhood. I was four or five years old and playing with neighbor kids, some my age, some older. One of the older kids asked if I knew about dinosaurs. I did. I knew they were huge, bigger than houses, and lived a long time ago and were not around anymore. The yard where we were playing had a small—maybe three feet by five feet—rectangular fishpond made of poured concrete. This older boy pointed into the pond and yelled, "There's a dinosaur coming out!" I was so scared I tore home as fast as I could because I was sure a dinosaur bigger than a house was coming out of that tiny pond. I still have a mental image of that beast in my memory—I see it, big and green, trampling over houses in the neighborhood. I cried and trembled until my mother assured me that there were no dinosaurs left in the world and that the neighbor boy was teasing, playing a trick on me. I continued, "The line between imagination and reality can, at times, blur."

Of course, that was her point!

I tried to explain that the fact that I remember this speaks to how rare it was for me to confuse my imagination with reality. The incident stands out.

She politely nodded but gave the look that implied that was not an answer.

"Fear," another student offered. "Doesn't fear screw with our minds?" A little crude but right. It was certainly true for me—dinosaurs trampling houses.

Not only fear, but any intense emotion or desire can intensify our imaginations to the point of distorting logic and realism. Dreaming of wealth, lottery players are sure they can beat the statistical odds and actually win. Or falling in love can be a kind of possession, a madness as Plato once argued. But fear likely tops the list of emotions that lead children and adults alike to confuse ideas and thoughts with reality. This is what Alison Bourchier and Alyson Davis found in their review of the research into what are called, coolly, "pretense-reality errors," studies that explore the conditions under which children make poor judgments about what is real and what is pretend.

First of all, it's not that common. But when confusion occurs, fear indeed is often the factor. Children are asked to imagine a pretend monster is in a box they know is empty. They are then hesitant or afraid to put their hands inside even though they know the monster is a figment of their own imaginations. In other words, some pretend premises or stipulations evoke emotions. Perhaps this is not so different from an adult crying over the protagonist's death in a novel or yelling for delight when a film character saves the day. Nonetheless, even under conditions of intense emotion, children more often than not still do not mistake reality and fantasy. Most will self-regulate their fear: they'll remind themselves the situation is pretend, or they'll use fantasy to create security: my magic glove will protect me from the monster biting. Context matters too. Present a transparent box and ask children to imagine a monster inside and they will be less likely to fear the contents. The fact that they can actually see that there is no monster makes it easier not to fear a pretend one. Reversing the logic, it is probably no coincidence that most scary monsters show up at night, when it is dark. Or they are hidden under a bed or in a closet, where there is no visual evidence to contradict the imagination.

Another factor is simply individual difference. Some children seem to be more credulous than others, especially in the absence of perceptual information. My young self was certainly quite gullible in the dinosaur-in-the-pond situation. Fear may have ramped up the credulity as well. But it could have been the other way around. I bought into the possibility because I was gullible, and then I was frightened to tears when I thought another kid saw a dinosaur in the darkness of the pond. It could be that some children are naturally credulous or naturally skeptical, having a disposition that leans more in one direction than the other. I also suspect that the degree of vividness of mental images could be another factor accounting for individual differences. This is less about gullibility and more about the intensity of the imagination. Studies with adults have certainly found individual differences in the vividness and intensity of mental imagery, dreams, and memories. It could be that children who experience mental images vividly are more likely to make reality-pretense mistakes.

Nonetheless, these are the exceptions that highlight the general rule. Children, even very young children, are remarkably skilled at differentiating make-believe from reality.

"Yep," I affirmed, "fear can screw with our minds."

About the same time I was traipsing around the Mayan ruins of the Yucatán, I discovered a beautiful book called *Born on a Blue Day*, a memoir by Daniel Tammet. I've been assigning it to classes ever since as a powerful illustration of the ways someone could be gifted in one realm of intelligence and challenged in others. Tammet is a savant with numbers, setting the world record for reciting the number π (3.1415926535 . . .) from memory to over twenty-two thousand digits. It took over five hours and lots of bananas and chocolate to do so. Professor Harvey would have loved Tammet—he has a form of synesthesia in which calculations appear as graphic figures in his mind. At the same time, he is on the autism spectrum, and the book describes the many frustrations and misunderstandings he encountered as a child.

Like the rest of the parental and psychological community, I have become increasing aware of the autism spectrum and some of the implications and complications for people on it. While there are many competing theories for its source, as well as vast individual differences, a common thread seems to be difficulty with understanding the invisible world of other minds. Expert on the subject, Simon Baron-Cohen calls it *mindblindness*. "Imagine what your world would be like," he writes, "if you were aware of physical things but were blind to the existence of mental things." The mental things he speaks of are thoughts, beliefs, and knowledge, for example, or the attitudes, intentions, and desires that motivate our behavior. The expectations about the world of people that most kids are born with don't come so intuitively. Tammet himself identifies as having Asperger syndrome, a high-functioning form of autism. And as gifted with numbers as he is, when it comes to understanding people with their *mental things*, Tammet struggled as a child and to some degree still struggles as an adult.

Pretending is one of the realms that confused the young Daniel. He describes hearing the story "Stone Soup" in school and being baffled. In the story, a soldier comes to a village and says he can make a delicious stone soup with nothing but water and stones. "Of course, stone soup with cabbage is hard to beat," the soldier declares. The villagers bring cabbage. And in the same way they bring meat, and then potatoes, and carrots, and onions, and more to make a wonderful soup. Tammet says he found the story very puzzling as a child "and did not understand that the soldier was pretending to make a soup from a stone in order to trick the villagers into contributing to it."

Tammet is not alone on this front. Children with autism generally find pretense difficult to comprehend and rarely, if ever, engage in pretend play themselves. In recalling his nursery (preschool) years, Tammet remembers: "There was the sandbox in which I spent long periods of the day picking and pulling at the sand, fascinated by the individual grains. Then came a fascination with hourglasses (the nursery had several of different sizes) and I remember watching the trickling, grainy flow of sand over and over again, oblivious to the children playing around me." He goes on to describe how in his first months in the preschool, he was taken by the different textures of the floor. There were mats in some places, carpet in others. "I remember walking slowly, my head firmly down, watching my feet, as I trod around the different parts of the floor, experiencing the different sensations under my soles."

If intense emotion can send the imagination of some children into overdrive and generate confusion, a hyperrealistic orientation can create its own brand of mix-up. At a time when many children are turning sticks into combs or dolls into babies, the young Daniel Tammet was absorbed by the world known through the senses. He says that he was not interested in the world of toys, that if he did hold a stuffed animal, there were no attempts at hugging it or cuddling. And what was true for toys was true for the social world in general.

Not only was Tammet emotionally cool with stuffed animals, he found the everyday interactions with classmates challenging. He explains how other children would *try* to talk with him. "I say 'try' because it was difficult for me to interact with them. For one thing, I did not know what to do or say. I almost always looked down at the floor as I spoke and did not think to try to make eye contact." Conversation from his side was a challenge as well, since he talked to others in long, uninterrupted sequences. "The idea of pausing or of taking turns in a conversation just did not occur to me." He writes, "I would talk, in very great detail, until I had emptied myself of everything that I wanted to say and felt that I might burst if I was interrupted in mid-flow. It never occurred to me that the topic I was talking about might not be of interest to the other person." To miss mental things means to miss many of the visible social cues that result from invisible thoughts and desires, such as fidgeting or looking around.

Daniel Tammet's great trials in the areas of pretense and social life set in relief how easily these realms of life come to most children, children who easily share conversations and interests with others. As an adult, Tammet has come to appreciate his differences and their challenges, has learned about social cues and deep friendship and the give and take of love. But the ability to easily, intuitively tune into the minds of others is still a challenge for him.

I believe Tammet's story also offers another clue to imaginary friends. If pretense is related to the social understanding of mental things, then so are pretend friends. Mental things, whether in visible or invisible friends, are see-through. The mind of another is intuited, inferred, implied, known indirectly, and has to be read from visible cues and behaviors in visible friends. If some children like Daniel have trouble doing so, others may be so intuitive or gifted at doing so that they don't even need the visible cues.

Another imaginary friend, Anne: "She was a very tall woman, more than six feet in height, and covered from head to toe in a long blue cloak. Her face was very thin and creased with wrinkles, because she was very, very old—more than a hundred years of age." Remarkably, this description comes from Daniel Tammet. He is remembering back to older childhood, his grade school days, and how Anne was one of several invisible friends who would accompany him on walks in the playground. She had a complex backstory: She was happily married to a blacksmith, John, but they never had children. Anne told Daniel she was grateful for his company. "We talked about my love of ladybirds and my coin towers, about books, about numbers, about tall trees and the giants and princesses of my favorite fairy tales." Tammet describes a particularly powerful moment with Anne. He asked her why he was so different from other children. She wouldn't answer directly but told him not to worry, that he would be fine. "A lot of what she said to me was meant as reassurance and it always worked, because when I left her I always felt happy and peaceful inside." That's a life-giver.

Tammet looks back on his relationships with imaginary friends as compensation for his sense of isolation, itself the result of challenges with (visible) friendships. Piaget and Freud would be happy with the interpretation. I don't doubt some children use imaginary relationships to compensate for loneliness. But with Daniel Tammet, I think something more is going on, more than compensation or splitting or genius or retinal images. Anne and these invisible friends emerged as his awareness of mental things became clearer. His early life was characterized by a hyperrealism attentive to the sense-based world. But once he gained some facility to relax his thoughts and attention from the detailed textures and sights of his environments, a tesseract opened the universe of imagination. In it he can practice the give and take rhythms of friendship, a logic that serves him well among the visible as well.

What if all life-givers are saints,

And Anne is a life-giver,

Then, is Anne a saint?

CHAPTER 4

SHARING

Well! I've often seen a cat without a grin," thought Alice; "but a grin without a cat! It's the most curious thing I ever saw in my life!"

I RECEIVED AN EMAIL from Deborah, a woman I know from church, the mother of two boys. Solomon was four years old at the time, and Neil was eight. Deborah, a journalist who had recently turned novelist, confessed that she had always been a little disappointed that the boys had shown no signs of having imaginary friends. But then the note: *In August before last we went on a camping trip and they started talking about "Baby Bear," a tiny creature who they built a home for out of sticks and carried around with them places. Neil at one point said: "Solomon, when you started this Baby Bear stuff, I thought, 'Oh brother.' But actually it is kind of fun."* The email went on to explain: *Since then, Baby Bear has made lots of appearances in our life, particularly when traveling. (Including on the camping trip last August.) This week, Solomon mentioned in passing that Baby Bear often goes to school with him. He said that when he goes down the steps, he doesn't take the steps, but a special invisible slide. He said: "He can use invisible things, since he's invisible." For some reason, it was only when he said that that I realized that Baby Bear was an imaginary friend, despite not being, you know, human.*

Within a week, I was in their home interviewing the boys. Each had drawn a picture of Baby Bear to share with me and each delighted in telling me about this otherwise invisible friend. I spoke with each boy separately. Solomon, the four-year-old, showed me his drawing, one with Baby Bear waving, and with reasonable pride he told me how he was able to write the friend's name. Then Solomon mentioned school.

I asked, "You bring Baby Bear to school? Where does Baby Bear stay while you're in school? Is he with you? Do you hide him, or—?"

"Well, his school is in my classroom." Solomon explained. "And his playground is like right under my playground."

"Ah, it's underneath your playground?" I echoed.

"Yeah, they look exactly the same, except for smaller."

Soon I was talking to his older brother, Neil, separately, while Solomon played in a nearby room. "You also kind of play with Baby Bear?" I asked Neil, "Or you watch your brother play with Baby Bear?" I was trying to get a firsthand feel for the attitude this eight-year-old took toward such see-through play. Would he be shy about it, embarrassed, other? I wanted to tread carefully with an eight-year-old's state of mind about imaginary play.

Neil said, "Normally, Baby Bear doesn't do anything whatsoever if we're not both together—"

From the other room Solomon, who had clearly been listening, shouted, "He's still in the family room playing!" The implication was that Baby Bear was with Solomon at that moment. A bit of brotherly rivalry on the issue, I suppose. Apparently Baby Bear could be with Solomon without Neil, but not the other way around.

Even so, Neil went on to tell me how they met Baby Bear in Acadia National Park in Maine. He showed me a photograph of twigs and rocks that his father had taken, and explained, "At the campsite, we got a bunch of rocks and sticks and tried to put together a little place for Baby Bear, a little tent [made of sticks]. I think we took this picture before we made the little campfire area. We had a little circle of stones with tiny sticks in there."

As I studied the photo, I admired the way the boys had copied their own campsite for their invisible friend. I thought about the way Baby Bear was discovered in a national park with bears and how he had his own playground under the school playground and took an invisible slide instead of stairs. These boys had created an alternative "little" world for Baby Bear, one reflecting their own, but with variation, like looking into a funhouse mirror. I admired as well, how Neil, four years his brother's elder, described playing along with Solomon, sharing so fully in the story of Baby Bear. He revealed no hint of parody, irony, embarrassment, or disdain in his voice. "It is kind of fun!"

I was touched by the sweetness of these siblings, four years apart, sharing an imaginary friend and creating a visible setting for him made of twigs and stones. Even the dispute about whom Baby Bear could do

Baby Bear (Neil's drawing)

Baby Bear (Solomon's drawing)

what with was playful. Beyond the sweetness, they moved me to wonder about the sheer mechanics of creating an imaginary friend together, the coordination of two children's minds to invest a third mind with life and personality. Perhaps these children of a novelist are indeed gifted with mental things, mind stuff with which they usher to life characters, settings, and plots like their mother does. Still, I'm amazed by the sharing. Nobody, not Mom or Dad, made them do it. They spontaneously played and shared. It was kinda fun. How does that happen?

A couple of years earlier, Jane and I were sitting in a Panera Bread restaurant, waiting for our soup and sandwiches to come up, when a little girl in a stroller caught our attention. She was looking at Jane, smiling behind her transparent pacifier. Suddenly, still holding Jane's eye, the girl pulled the pacifier out of her mouth and held it up high to show her, as if to say, "Look here, isn't this thing great?" We were all smiling at this point.

"How old do you think she is?" I asked Jane.

"Maybe six or seven months," she said.

"I think at least nine," I was not overly confident. She was small. But I had been reading about the "nine-month revolution" in a book by Michael Tomasello called *The Cultural Foundations of Human Cognition*. Somewhere between nine and twelve months, most children begin to engage in what he calls *joint attention*. They point to a bird or hold up a pacifier to get others to share the view with them: "Look!" The revolution is a remarkable developmental achievement and represents an evolutionary milestone as well.

Tomasello has been studying primates for over three decades, from monkeys and gorillas to chimpanzees and those strangest of all great apes, *Homo sapiens*. He is particularly interested in how primates think and describes all kinds of complex cognitive abilities going on, not only among humans but among nonhuman primates as well: remembering locations, knowing where food is and which fruits will ripen when, using simple tools, learning from others, recognizing individuals, problem solving, and using gestures or sounds to communicate. Other great apes—chimpanzees particularly—are deeply social creatures as well. They align with others for protection, have a level of self-awareness, monitor their own behavior, and may even cooperate under certain circumstances.

But one thing the nonhuman apes don't do. They don't invite joint attention. They don't hold up objects or point to them. Only humans do that, invite a shared view, and they do so as early as nine months of age. Before nine months, babies tend to interact with people or objects in dyads—that is, in a one-on-one, back-and-forth way. If a six-month-old is examining a ball and you hand him a block, he puts down the ball. If you make a funny face, he looks at you and ignores the ball or block altogether. Attention is dyadic. But with the revolution, triads emerge. The one-year-old notices where you are looking, maybe at a dog walking by, and follows your gaze to see what's going on. Children can begin to sync their attention to that of others, or they try to get others to sync attention with theirs.

"Excuse me," Jane said to the little girl's mother, "what a delightful child."

"Thanks," the mother said.

"And how old is she?"

"She just turned ten months."

The order came up and I brought our sandwiches back to the table. "I'm impressed," Jane said to me, referring to my age-guessing skills.

"I cheated," I confessed and told her about the revolution.

As I reflected on Baby Bear, this shared invisible friend, I began considering pretend friends in the light of the revolution. A theme was emerging: *sharing.* Sharing the view is key to understanding mental things. I can see now why the theme was forming when it did. As I was listening to stories about Quack-Quack and Baby Bear, I was completing a book about the deeply social roots of the human mind. *Original Knowing* follows an evolutionary trail into our hominid past to find clues to the emergence of the kind of mind that writes books and computer code, sings and dances with others, builds space stations and Gothic cathedrals, or trades information and symbolic currency. That trail led through joint attention to a mind that easily cooperates, that intentionally informs, shares knowledge, accumulates information, and builds upon it. As I began to consider the phenomenon of imaginary friends through the looking glass of sharing, I could see something profoundly human going on, something deeply social. Tomasello calls it the *we-mode*—because the human ape not only shares views in physical space but shares views in mental space.

Mental space: the territory where ideas, purposes, hopes, goals, information, desires, and more dwell and animate our lives. Invisible yet no less real for its intangibility, it rests somewhere beneath our actions and movements, behind the behaviors of our bodies and the products of our hands. But where is that exactly? Behind the eyes in our brains? Too literal. Too hard to share. Besides, we seem to live in this invisible realm as much as it lives in us. No, the precise location of this ghostly world, we can only imagine. Yet even young children find it. They can put their minds together to accomplish a common purpose—say, to build a campsite for an imaginary friend. Creating a joint purpose is the heart of cooperation, a shared view in mental space that lives not only in my mind or yours but fashions a site where both camp. Children are born into this invisible world as surely as they are delivered into a world of textures and sounds. As they coordinate their bodies to learn to walk in physical space, they also coordinate their minds in the land of invisibles.

Last night I dreamed about our granddaughter, Elly. She's eight weeks old today, as I write. We were in a restaurant, and I was carrying her in my arms towards a table where the extended family was gathering. She started talking. I was surprised because of course she's too young to do much more than gurgle or cry. She likely won't even babble for a few more months. I listened to her in the dream, tickled by her speaking, and realized it was not a language I've heard before; yet the speech had the rhythm and structure of a language. It dawned on me in this dream that she had made up her own!

Language in humans is one of those features of cognition that requires sharing mental space. As amazing as a baby inventing a language would be, it would not work very well if nobody else knew what the words meant. The notion that words mean something—that they represent people or objects, actions or even ideas—requires a mental partnership. For example, you and I share the idea that the word *home* refers to a place where people live, *up* is the space above us, *walking* refers to a way of moving our bodies with our legs. If I say, "Let's *flitzboti*," you'd be lost because we don't share the view that gives the word meaning. There is no triad because I made it up (actually Elly did, in the dream, and I don't know what it means either).

The dream reminded me of Cora as a toddler, when she was learning words, learning to share the mental view that gives language life. We played a little game at the dinner table. "Cora, can you say *Daddy*?"

And she would echo, "Da-da." She did the same for Mommy ("Mama") and her brother David ("Day-day"). I would even ask her if she could say *Cora*, "Co-wah."

We continued to play our little name game over the next several evenings. As before, with each prompt she repeated our names, as well as her own, "Co-wah." Then one night a change occurred. She repeated our names when prompted, but when I asked, "Can you say *Cora*?"—nothing. She looked puzzled, and so did we. The next few evenings yielded the same: she would repeat our names, but when it came to her own, nothing.

Then another shift occurred. After asking about our names, I asked, "Can you say *Cora*?" This time she smiled and declared, "Me!"

In the midst of learning words, children learn that some words are not so simple. The word *me*, for example, can refer to lots of people, to whoever uses it, and Cora no doubt had heard us do so: "Pass the peanut butter to me." "Give me a hug." She would have heard the word in books, on television, and from others outside the family as well. To use the word to refer to herself, she had to appreciate that *me* was not restricted to any one particular person or object but had a flexible quality, depending upon the context, much as a popsicle stick could be a comb or spoon. The word could refer even to herself. It could be used to represent her own intentions and desires to others and to herself. I had asked her if she could say *Cora*, but she answered with *me*. She was not imitating; she was imagining herself.

A child represents herself to herself, sharing the view of herself with herself. Amazing. I think of the famous drawing by M. C. Escher, *Drawing Hands*. Each hand is drawing the other into existence. In the process, possibilities are born. If Cora can imagine herself, she can imagine doing this or doing that, saying yes or saying no. A profound sense of her own agency is drawn into her existence—agency with flexibility, autonomy.

Cora had wandered into that strange land of shared mental space, where sounds become words, and where some words could mean one thing here and another there, and some of those words could be as reflexive as a looking glass, referring back to the user. And there she was, *me*! Before long Cora began investing stuffed animals and dolls with a *me* as well, coupling agency—those invisible thoughts, desires, emotions, and motivations that animate people—to otherwise inanimate objects. "Dolly is sleepy now." A year later she could even attribute a *me* to a friend nobody could see, coupling those invisible aspects of agency not only to a visible doll but to otherwise empty space. "Crystal wants a cookie."

Baby Bear, a pacifier, a sweet dream, Cora learning words. I could see imaginary friends growing in the soil of revolution, of sharing views. So important is sharing the view to the human mind that kids will do it even when nobody's around. Some, like Neil and Solomon, will do so together.

"Is Baby Bear still around?" Nearly five years after the interview I had an email conversation with Deborah and thought to ask.

She wrote back, "I just asked Solomon how Baby Bear was doing, since I had not heard him mentioned in a while and Solomon said, 'he's doing great, but I haven't talked to him in a while.' I asked if he went on vacation with us." She explained that they had just taken their first non-camping vacation, to London, and wondered. Deborah reported that "he said that Baby Bear did [go with them] and he really liked it. I'm not sure what this means exactly, because I don't remember him being mentioned, but it suggests that Baby Bear is still important in some way."

It did not surprise me that Deborah, a novelist, would appreciate that a fictional character discovered in the forests of Maine was important to her children. The lush forest of mental space is densely populated with characters, some based on people we have known, others invented by storytellers who use books and films to establish them in our hearts. Even when we know a story is fiction, we get attached. I think of one of the first interviews we conducted, the same day we interviewed Nathan with Quack-Quack and his other "pretend friends," as he called them. I borrowed the term when I spoke with a little girl, Jennifer, and her mother. "And what's the name of the pretend friend again?" It was a rookie mistake.

"Um," Mom paused for a moment, then spoke very quietly. "The last time we used that phrase there was a meltdown." Jennifer was thoughtful enough to simply ignore my comment this time. It was clear from the interview that Jennifer knew the friends were pretend—she wasn't confused. At the same time, she didn't want anyone diminishing their importance, her attachment to them. Someone had apparently used the term in a condescending way: "Come on, they're just pretend." I could imagine myself shedding a tear over a favorite character in a novel and someone saying, "Come on, it's just a story." I might have a meltdown too.

Characters may be imaginary but the feelings are genuine. When we share the view for any length of time, even with made-up figures, we get attached. As characters in stories stir us, as children care about imaginary friends, something deep in the hominid soul is at work. Inevitably the attachments of our hearts come and go, transform or reappear. Stella dies, Flower Barbie shows up. Harry Potter lives but could die. Romeo and Juliet love each other and both die. Coda dies but comes back. The worlds of fiction and of imaginary friendships reflect the rhythms of the heart in a fragile world, engage our emotional lives, offer characters we care about, and perhaps even change how we understand one another. Yes, Baby Bear is still important.

"Her mouth was clamped tightly closed and her face was softer and brighter than the few occasions that I had seen it before close-up." Daniel Tammet is here describing a fateful day with his wise, very old imaginary friend, Anne. "She did not say anything for several minutes and then she spoke very, very softly and slowly and told me that she had to go and could not return." Daniel became very upset, wanting to know why. She told him "that she was dying and was here to say good-bye." She disappeared, and Tammet says he cried and cried until he couldn't cry anymore.

What if, I wondered as this theme of sharing took shape, imaginary characters offer practice for navigating the strange territory of shared views, of shared mind, of shared hearts? I thought back several years to a time the great children's book author Katherine Paterson was on our campus. She was talking about her Newbery Medal–winning book *Bridge to Terabithia*, a beautiful, tragic story of friendship between two children, Jess and Leslie, a friendship ruptured when Leslie suddenly and accidentally drowns. Paterson was telling us on this day how so many people report that they have given the book to children after they too had lost someone they love. Paterson said that when she hears this, she thinks to herself, "That's nice, but too late." For her, *Bridge* and other tales of loss do their best work beforehand, before tragedy strikes. The soul needs preparation to face pain and death.

Perhaps invisible friends and imagined characters are tilling the soil of our hearts, prepping the soul for love and loss. In a way, they allow us to run simulations of shared life, of relationships. As cognitive psychologists point out, people are relentless simulators, model makers. Toy trains and dolls, model cars and little campsites. And we make invisible mental models as well, maps that distill the stuff of the world so that we can work with it. Stories do the same; they take key features of places and people to create simulations—settings and characters—in mental space. They distill and compress and focus our attention on what matters.

As I write, I notice my grandmother's copy of Frank Baum's *The Wizard of Oz* resting on a bookshelf. It's a hardcover, green with black and gold lettering, copyright 1899 (but this is a 1903 edition), with illustrations. Inside she has scratched out her older brother's name, Wofford, and entered her own, Cora Nell, in the handwriting of a child. I open to the first page of the story. "Dorothy lived in the midst of the great Kansas prairies, with Uncle Henry, who was a farmer, and Aunt Em, who was a farmer's wife." We see only Dorothy's back as she looks out to the horizon. The first sentence takes us right to the characters and place that constitute *home*, the people of Dorothy's heart, the land she will soon desperately miss. It does not catalogue each species of prairie grass, all the varieties of trees, the number of leaves on each tree in Kansas, the number of boards and nails used to build the house, or the infinite number of things that could be described. Instead, Baum goes on to describe the house where they live and the cyclone cellar beneath, both of which are critical to the drama to come.

In this way, fiction creates a simulation of experience, a mental model of a world much like our own, to start, but opens to the unworldly possibilities of talking scarecrows and flying witches. What gets our interest in the story is desire, the hopes and dreams of a few characters to whom we will get attached as Dorothy, the main character, gets attached to them. The scarecrow wants a brain, the tin woodsman a heart, the lion courage, and of course Dorothy wants to get back home to Kansas. There are helpers and adversaries along the way, but overcoming the obstacles to these desires, through cooperation, drives the story. In the end, the more we identify with the imaginary characters, the greater joy we feel when obstacles are removed and desires are fulfilled. Dorothy arrives home, grateful to be there. We are too.

I put the book back in its place, carefully, as the binding is failing after a hundred years of use. I imagined my grandmother as a little girl reading the tale, wanting along with the characters a brain, a heart, and courage. I thought of her, together with a century's worth of other children, learning from Dorothy that *friendship* and *home*—those attachments of our lives—are more meaningful, if not more powerful, than anything a wizard could offer. Given all the complexities and ambiguities of our deeply social minds, of sharing views, stories may well help train us in the invisible arts of human relationships. By creating a simulation of friendships and enemies in Oz, Baum gives readers insight into the minds of others, their desires and dreams, hopes and fears. I suspect that in turn Cora Nell understood human characters a little better for having traveled with imaginary ones. And I find myself both less surprised but more impressed that some children find their own invisible characters with whom to explore hearts, brains, and courage.

"So, Dad, what can you tell me about the imaginary companions?" Lacey Ryan, another interviewer with the project, had just finished talking with five-year-old Ruth in their home. Ruth was nearby, drawing a picture of her two invisible friends: George, who was six years old, and the other one, a seven-year-old girl who was also named Ruth.

Invisible Ruth lived "next door," but at that moment both invisible Ruth and invisible George were sitting in the room alongside visible Ruth as Lacey spoke with her father.

John, the dad, answered, "Well I'd heard about George before, but I had not heard about Ruth until today."

Visible Ruth, overhearing the conversation offered, "They come to the house whenever I ask them to."

"So they don't come over," Lacey clarified, "without being invited?"

"No."

"Well, that's very polite of them," Lacey commented. She turned back to Dad and asked what he knew of George.

"Um, she just mentions him in play and maybe when saving a seat for him at the table." With this, Ruth chuckled a little bit.

Lacey asked Ruth, "Does he like to eat with you?"

"Yes."

Listening to this interview, I was reminded of the big bang theory. Not the one that describes the origins of the cosmos 13.8 billion years ago but one that accounts for the emergence of the *big mind* of humans 2 to 3 million years ago. Food is involved. William Calvin, author of *A Brief History of the Mind*, describes a couple of big bangs, times of relatively rapid brain growth, with evidence for leaps of corresponding mind growth. One is 2.5 million years ago with the proliferation of toolmaking, simple stone choppers. They were used to crack open the bones of scavenged animal carcasses, allowing easier access to the calorie-rich marrow inside. With choppers, our ancestors could even wait until the lion had already picked all the meat off the bones and still get a great meal. Another growth occurs a half million years ago. Tools proliferate in number and variety. Group size increases as well, implying increasingly complex social interactions. These ancestors traveled, living on and off the African continent. And they were making fires.

Nobody knows for sure, but it is likely that these growth spurts were accompanied by big bangs in cooperation and social complexity among our ancestors. It may have begun simply, out of desperation for diminishing resources. Maybe some reciprocal scavenging—I'll let you work off this carcass today so you'll let me do the same tomorrow—or group foraging or hunting. Perhaps sharing food was an extension of parenting; giving food to offspring led to sharing with kin or allies. But it is not hard to imagine eating was involved. Some hungry hominids put their heads together to find food and blossomed into the kind of creature that cooperates regularly, that informs, helps, shares, and over the generations, accumulates knowledge for millennia.

After a pause, Lacey asked John, Ruth's father, "Is there anything else about George?"

"Well, lately her sister has been talking more about an imaginary friend named George." Ruth's sister, Sarah, was three years old at the time. Sarah was in another room, along with her mother, Eva, being interviewed by Katrina Paxson, also a member of the research team.

Katrina set up the recorder and said to young Sarah, "This is just going to let me know what we say. Is that cool?"

"That *is* cool," the three-year-old answered with an emphasis suggesting she had never encountered such a device before.

"That *is* cool," Katrina repeated with the same emphasis. Then Katrina asked whether she had a friend from school or from the neighborhood. It was a way of warming up to talking about invisible friends, and something we did in every interview.

Sarah named a friend, and explained, "We like to play mommies and babies." The other reason for asking about these friends (the visible kind) is that it helps set up the contrast with invisible ones.

Katrina said, "And now some friends are different, maybe ones that other people can't see. Do you have a friend like that?" She did. Like her sister's, her friend was George. "Can you tell me, where is George right now?"

"Um, with his—" she interrupts herself, "—he's eating breakfast with his friend with the yellow hat. Because, you know he loves bananas, so maybe he's having banana cereal." The food theme again, even in a different room and with a different parent.

"Can you tell me a little bit about George?"

"He loves bananas, he's curious; he loves climbing on things; he loves all kind of things."

Katrina realized Sarah was describing the character in the Hans and Margret Rey *Curious George* picture books as well as a television cartoon series. "Can you draw me a picture of George?" Sarah agreed, and Katrina handed her paper and crayons. "You can draw on that table over there while I talk to your mom a little bit." That sounded good to Sarah, and Katrina helped her carry the crayons and paper to the table. But along the way one of the crayons fell to the carpet. Katrina pointed this out: "I think we dropped a crayon."

Sarah stopped and said, "Ah, that crayon is curious!" This made Katrina laugh. Sarah had just granted a mind, a *me*, agency, to a crayon, a *me* with the desire to jump out of Katrina's hand out of curiosity like George's in order to explore the world of the carpet.

Sarah settled in at the table, and while she drew, Katrina asked Mom about George. Eva explained that in addition to Curious George the monkey, there's a George that Sarah plays with at the playground. "She pushes George on the swing, and she talks to George and lets George know if we're going to move on and play somewhere else. And she sometimes tells jokes with George and thinks they're really funny." Eva paused a moment, wanting to make the status of this friend very clear. "But I've never *seen* the George we play with at the park."

Sarah walked over with a drawing. "This is him saying *ooh-ooh, ah-ah!*" It was her best impersonation of a monkey. "You can keep it." This was monkey George.

Katrina asked Sarah if she could draw another picture, and Sarah obliged, giving Katrina another chance with Mom.

"How long has George been around?"

Eva thought a while. It had been about a year for Sarah, since she was two and a half. But George had been around even longer, with her sister Ruth. Sometimes they played together with George, but each would play with George on her own.

Katrina asked, "Did you have one when you were little?"

"I did," Eva answered, a bit sheepish about it. "I had one. It was a boy named Ricky. We moved a lot, but Ricky moved with us—every time we moved—when I was a little kid."

Sarah came back with another drawing and started talking about her other *little monkeys*, besides George. "One time when I was playing musical chairs, I couldn't find Brown Monkey. And Blue Monkey and Brown Monkey love to stay together." This was getting to be a lot of Georges and a lot of monkeys.

And even Mom was getting fuzzy about who was who. "What about the one that sits at dinner with us? Remember, sometimes you pull up a chair for him?"

Sarah explained that playground George was the one who ate with them. So in addition to sharing George in play, the sisters shared George at meals with the whole family.

"I just think it's fun when George is around. How about you?" Mom asked Sarah. Yes, it sure was.

"Where is that [playground] George right now?" asked Katrina.

"Napping somewhere."

"Is he friends with George the monkey [aka Curious George]?"

Sarah laughed, then offered, "George the monkey is nowhere! It's only on TV."

<hr>

What a strange concept, *nowhere*, especially out of the mouth of a three-year-old child. Nowhere: a place that is not any place, is not firm like swing sets and houses, and is closely related to the pretend world of television monkeys. This little girl demonstrated the double knowledge that works on two levels at the same time: the realm of playgrounds and dinner tables as well as the realm of fictional animated characters and invisible monkeys pushed in a swing. Nowhere and somewhere intertwined, visible and invisible, seen and unseen, imaginary and sensed, a world that is and a world that could be, even if *nowhere*.

I would later discover more children who not only played together with invisible friends but ate together with them. Whether I should or not, it is difficult for me not to see a connection between a child breaking bread with an invisible friend and the deep origins of the human mind in food sharing. But in this instance, it is even harder for me not to see a connection between Ruth and Sarah's family setting a place at the table for George and the fact that their father is a theologian. His focus is upon Christian worship and the sacraments, especially the ritual of Communion. Sharing bread in the context of worship has something to do with a life of sharing, with holding communities together, with love itself. With a *little* bread and *little* wine, it's as if communities are creating models, much as Neil and Solomon made a *little* campsite with *little* stones and twigs. It's as if worshipping communities are running simulations to visibly express invisible realities.

If it is true that the roots of the unique aspects of human knowing may grow from sharing food, perhaps saving a seat for invisible friends, maybe the ritual eating practiced in religions across the globe should not be so surprising. We do know meals have gathered friends, families, and communities for millennia, as long as words have recorded history. As have the gods. People gather to praise, pray, sing, inform, and often eat together. Religions around the world incorporate food into the celebration of life, share food with those who need it, and in some cases, the food becomes a god. Along with drink. In many traditions, wherever mortals mingle with the sacred, you will find fermented drinks—from a hymn praising the Sumerian goddess Ninkasi for making beer to the wedding at Cana, where Jesus turns vats of water into wine, and from the Passover Kiddush to the wine festivals of Greece celebrating Dionysus, sharing a sacred cup generates holy praise.

Food and drink are an outward and visible sign of invisible sharing.

I had been working with the interviews about Baby Bear all week when I experienced a surprising synchronicity. It was Holy Week, which had allowed a few days' break from the classroom and time for writing. Seven years had passed; Solomon and Neil were eleven and fifteen years old. Now it was Easter and Solomon was up front in church with another child, Mary, eight years old, helping the pastor with Communion. The church often involves children in worship—pouring baptismal water, lighting a candle, singing—but helping with the Lord's Supper is not typical. The vision of the pastor and two children behind the table was striking.

"Why do we eat bread at this table?" Solomon asked, echoing the point in a Jewish Passover Seder (also this week) when a child asks, "Why on this night, only matzah?"

"Why do we eat bread?" The pastor responded to Solomon, "Because Jesus took the bread, blessed it, and gave it to his friends saying, 'This is my body broken for you.'"

Mary asked, "Why do we drink from the cup at this table?"

"Because," the pastor responded, "Jesus said, 'This is the new covenant, sealed in my blood.'"

When the service ended, the whole congregation recessed to the plaza outside the front doors of the building. For several years now, on Easter, the congregation has created a drum circle after the service to celebrate. "Resurrection rhythms" someone dubbed it. Instruments from all over the world come out—shakers that look like Easter eggs, djembes, tambourines, güiros, congas, bongos, doumbeks, tablas, and more. Rhythm makers from everywhere. And the kids love it. Neil and Solomon were both drumming. So was I.

The drumming ended after twenty or thirty minutes. In a sweat on this warm April day, I walked over to the family and said, "I've been thinking of you all week. I've been writing about Baby Bear." I looked at the boys, "I don't know if you remember, but I came to your house and you told me stories about Baby Bear."

Deborah asked her sons, "You remember Baby Bear?" Both nodded and smiled.

"I promise, it's sweet," I assured.

Deborah said, laughing a bit, "It's so nice to think that Baby Bear lives on."

CHAPTER 5

WILD MIND

*"I know who I was when I got up this morning,
but I think I must have been changed several times
since then."*

I OPEN THE CASE TO THE DVD—a Christmas present from my daughter—and pop the disk into the player. A big, haunted-looking house appears. Two animated figures, one a boy, the other a blue blob—ghostlike—with eyes, walk through a gate at the sidewalk and towards the house. They enter the building and all variety of wild characters, challenging to describe in words, move across the screen: a cluster of eyes with legs; a cute pink bear with a symbol of a heart on its belt; a purple witch's hat with spider legs; a glob of green slime with its tongue hanging out. This is just the menu screen. And even the buttons that say Play All, Episodes, and Set Up are characters. One is tapping its foot as if waiting for me to do something.

So I do. I hit Play All and I soon learn that the boy in the opening is eight-year-old Mac and the blob is his imaginary friend Bloo, short for Blooregard Q. Kazoo.

Because Bloo and Mac keep fighting with Mac's older brother, their mother decides it's time for Bloo to go, that Mac, at eight, is too old to have an imaginary friend: "You've got to get rid of Bloo." Well, Mac and Bloo are horrified, but that night while channel-surfing, Bloo sees an ad for Foster's Home for Imaginary Friends, which, according to the ad, "is a wonderful, funderful imagination habitation." The home will provide food, shelter, and a warm heart for imaginary friends. "So if you know of, or have, an imaginary friend that desperately needs a home, then come on down to Foster's Home for Imaginary Friends, where good ideas are not forgotten."

Before long, Bloo and Mac are at the door of Foster's Home and greeted by a giant bunny butler wearing a monocle, named Mr. Herriman. Characters galore run, bounce, and fly around—a tiny book on legs; a pair of glasses, with eyes, dashing across the room on its stems; a yellow flying ladybug-type creature with the face of a boy; a huge purple caterpillar with a flower for a tail, smoking a pipe and wearing sneakers on each foot; a flying octopus sporting a derby; and a pair of scissors on stork legs. These are only a few of the imaginary friends populating the home. Bloo thinks it's perfect, and with the condition that Mac visit every day, Bloo moves into his new home, and the adventures begin.

Foster's Home for Imaginary Friends was created by the Cartoon Network and ran for five years, from 2004 to 2009. But in 2014, the home and its characters reemerged in comic book form. And, as if playing with this genre-shifting, a new shapeshifting imaginary friend joined the gang, Pixel. Pixel appears as a robot at first but then takes on the shape of a purple, Spanish-speaking bull, then transforms into a bookstand (with reading lamp) before returning to his original robotness. The other characters are delighted with their new protean companion, and they all start preparing for the "adopt-a-thought" party the home is throwing, during which kids have the chance to adopt an imaginary friend.

In all, *Foster's Home* is clever and silly and wonderfully captures the unpredictable imaginations at work in children. Before this day, I had already been struck by the gender-bending, species-crossing forms of several invisible friends: Tea and Jeff/ette switched genders; Dino the dragon was sometimes a space alien; Cinderella was a little girl one day and a blue dog the next. But watching the cartoon intensified my curiosity.

~~~~~~~~~~~~~~~~~~~~

Among the children we interviewed, the champion of transformation was Lucy, invisible friend of three-year-old Sophia. Sophia had been interviewed by Lacey, and in her notes Lacey had jotted down "Shape-Shifter—changes forms."

According to Sophia's mother, Lucy had been around for nearly a year, "as soon as Sophia started making full sentences." The name, she thought, was likely taken from the *I Love Lucy* show and, like Lucy Ricardo near the end of the show's run, invisible Lucy was "a mom" at times, the mother of a daughter, Alice. Lucy and Alice were not always at home, but Sophia always knew where they were and could be in contact with them whenever she liked. According to Sophia's mother, a few days earlier Sophia had been on an old, unusable cell phone with Lucy for nearly forty-five minutes.

I remembered a wonderful article in the *New Yorker* from several years earlier. Adam Gopnik tells of his three-year-old daughter, Olivia, and her imaginary friend, Charlie Ravioli. The odd thing is that Charlie Ravioli is a "hero of busyness," too otherwise occupied to actually play with his daughter. "She holds her toy cell phone up to her ear, and we hear her talking into it: 'Ravioli? It's Olivia . . . It's Olivia. Come and play? O.K. Call me. Bye.' Then she snaps it shut, and shakes her head. 'I always get his machine,' she says." The article is part fascination with invisible friends and part commentary on the busy New York lifestyle of Olivia's parents.

I listened again to Lacey's recorded conversation with Sophia.

Lacey asked, "Can you tell me a little bit about Lucy? You said she has a head, a body, and feet? What else about Lucy?"

"Well," Sophia, explained, "her name is Lucy—you can spell it *c-l-c-l.*" Sophia was learning the alphabet and liked to practice spelling.

Lacey, unsure, asked, "*c-l-c-l*? What's that mean?"

Sophia clarified that she was spelling the name Lucy.

"Oh, okay. What else can you tell me about Lucy? What does Lucy look like?"

"A rabbit," answered Sophia. "I don't know how to spell that."

"That's okay," Lacey assured her. "I know how to spell it. Thank you though. Your mom mentioned that sometimes Lucy changes a little bit, changes into different animals?"

Sophia agreed.

"She does?" Lacey continued, "What animals does she become?"

"A lion and a tiger and a mouse."

"So she changes into all kinds of animals?"

Sophia paused, then added, "And a zebra."

"Oh." Lacey waited a moment. "Where is Lucy now?"

"She's at work."

"Where does she work?"

"Hmm." Sophia seemed to need time to consider the question but then offered, "She works at ABCs, because that's her work."

When I heard this on the recording, I wondered whether there was a store called ABC anywhere in town. I seemed to recall a convenience store by the same name somewhere I've lived, but I couldn't recall one in Louisville. As the recording continued, I realized I was on the wrong course.

Lacey asked, "She works at her ABCs, that's what she does?"

"Uh-huh." Then Sophia starts singing the "Alphabet Song," ending with "Tell me what you think of me."

"Very good. All right. Good job. So Lucy works at her ABCs like you?" Sophia agreed.

This little exchange between Lacey and Sophia could have come right out of a script for *Foster's Home for Imaginary Friends*. I can just imagine a cartoon rabbit transforming into a lion, then a tiger, and finally a zebra at a convenience store while singing her ABCs in a kind of pun about work. Perhaps this is part of the attraction of animation in general for children. Characters can transform and shift shapes as easily as if they were from a child's imagination. Yet, notably, through all the transformations, Lucy is still Lucy.

The closest analogy I can generate for an adult mind is dreaming. In a dream, I may see my brother Steve as a child playing in the room we shared growing up. Next we are walking down the street and Steve is a man. Then he doesn't even look like Steve anymore but like the waiter at the restaurant where I ate the night before. Yet somehow it's still Steve. In my dream mind, there is some essential "Steveness" about him throughout the transformations. A less dramatic version happens in the everyday waking mind as well. If Steve goes to a high school reunion and some old friends see him for the first time in thirty years, they will see, on the outside, a Steve who looks quite different from the seventeen-year-old Steve they once knew. But he is still Steve. The Steveness of my brother has more to do with an invisible something, a core, a self that endures through time and external variations. The form may change, but the Steve abides.

Without a sense that others have an essence, we could not even have the idea of a shapeshifter in the first place. It's likely related to our model-making minds that generate distilled simulations of the world around us. Trees will have certain properties underlying all the variations of them: trunks, roots, bark, leaves or needles. People will have other properties: heads, legs, arms, and so on. We have mental categories of stuff, types of things or creatures that make them what they are and differentiate them from other types—say, trees versus people. This can be very useful. If I learn that rattlesnake bites are poisonous, I will try to avoid them and certainly not pick up any rattlesnake. If a child cautiously tries a blueberry for the first time and likes it, she will assume that she will like the taste of any blueberry. She doesn't have to cautiously approach each one—at least until she tries a very firm, unripe one that is sour, and then she has to fine-tune her like of blueberries to exclude very firm ones. It is not difficult to see how our sense of kind or type serves us.

"Is it a skunk or a raccoon?" That's what cognitive psychologist Frank Keil asked children as a way to explore the ways they think about essences and categories. He told the children that doctors painted a raccoon black with a white stripe down its back and put stinky stuff all over it so that it smelled and looked like a skunk. So skunk or raccoon? What Kiel discovered was that age affected the answer children gave. Older children, six and up, said that the creature was still a raccoon even though it looked and smelled like a skunk. They understood that raccoonness is not only a matter of appearance but something more fundamental, some underlying essence unaffected by the changes. However, younger children tended to say that the creature had indeed become a skunk. Why? Because it looked and smelled like a skunk. That is, essences for young children are more flexible than they are for older children and adults. Perhaps this is why a three-year-old's imaginary friend could easily shift shapes and be a tiger or a lion or a rabbit.

But could Lucy be a cactus? Are there limits to this flexibility, even among preschoolers? In another study, children were told that doctors gave a porcupine something to make it sleep for a long time, so it couldn't move, and they painted it yellow green so that it looked like a cactus. The children were shown a picture of a cactus. "Is it a cactus or a porcupine?" In this case, even young preschoolers believed that the "cactus" was still actually a porcupine. Even three-year-olds have some sense of abiding essences, at the least when it comes to animalness verses plantness.

Is this another view from nowhere? The essence of a porcupine, even if it looks exactly like a cactus, comes from where? Visibility is not the essence of essence. And perhaps we can better see how children so effortlessly form relationships with invisible beings whether imaginary companions, grandfathers who have died, or even an invisible god.

It could be that Sophia was playing both sides of the essence card—flexible enough to switch animal forms, but the essence of Lucy was still Lucyness. But I think something else was going on, another kind of essentialism, one related to individuals. Lucy could still be Lucy, and my brother could still be my brother, despite appearances, because once someone becomes a unique person in our heart and mind, and not just part of a crowd—not just a type or kind—the game changes. That person, this individual, has an essence, something not reducible to a generic category. Each has a unique identity, a particular history, a distinct set of experiences. The Lucyness of Sophia's shapeshifting friend is the underlying continuity of an individual amid changes. That distilled Lucy can inhabit different types, dwell in the midst of more generic kinds of kinds—rabbits, moms, or zebras even.

So I dream of Steve still being my brother despite looking like last night's waiter. His Steveness reflects an abiding sense of his essence, a core that is not easily obscured despite appearances. Dreams keep such essences alive for us, those who may be gone from our waking lives—a grandparent who died, a childhood neighbor, a first love. It takes no great leap to see how religions and cultures around the world can speak of immortal souls, ancestor spirits, an afterlife, an enduring consciousness, ghosts, resurrection, or reincarnation, for example. In these is an assumption that some kind of essence of who we are endures.

But that is not the only connection between cognition—how our minds work—and religion. This core soul-sensing capacity is central to the moral life. Thinking in kinds and categories may serve us well enough when trying to differentiate a skunk from a raccoon or eat only the ripe blueberries. But the backside of this power is that we use categories and kinds too quickly, too easily, in relation to people. We not only type, but stereotype. We are tempted to turn others into kinds.

The great moral philosopher Martin Buber said that when we do this, we are reducing an I-Thou relationship into an I-It. We turn a You into an It, and that changes the character of the relationship from subject-subject to subject-object. In religious language, to turn a You into an It is to refuse to recognize the way others are made in the image of God, or to be blind to their Buddha nature, or to believe their kind doesn't have souls. It is to treat others as if they are nothing but this or that type rather than an irreducible Thou.

What if, I wonder, the shapeshifters of the imagination are helpers, there to open the mind and heart to irreducibility? Moral helpers even. Not so much like Jiminy Cricket voicing a conscience—I found scant evidence of this in our research—but more like loving friends or family whose very presence tenderizes our hearts, makes us mindful of others, tills the field for seeing through stereotypes. Through ordinary play, fun, and companionship, perhaps invisible friends disrupt the temptation to distill others into kinds alone, into Its, and in doing so make way for an awareness of more. George isn't just a monkey, he eats with us. Lucy is not only a mom or a tiger, but she works and sings her ABCs. There is always more to them than meets the eye. The point is all the more beautiful when they are invisible anyway. Invisible friends giving life to a sense of more, of Thou, of irreducibility. A big claim, purely speculative, but still I wonder.

Another shapeshifter, this one from Homer's *Odyssey*, is the god Proteus. The ship captain Meneláos and his sailors are stranded by weeks of calm winds off the shores of Egypt and have used up all their supplies. The only divine helper around is Proteus, the Ancient of the Salt Sea, but, Homer explains, he is an elusive god, not interested in face-to-face encounters with sailors. Yet, as the sea-nymph and daughter of Proteus, Eidothea, explains, if they can catch him by surprise and hold on, they will be able to wrestle the help they need from him. It will not be easy, "for he can take the forms of all the beasts, and water, and blinding fire."

In honor of the sea god, the word *protean* means "changeable," "fluid," "unpredictable," "unexpected," "unsettled," "inconsistent," "mercurial," or "kaleidoscopic." The stuff of dreams. The stuff of imaginary friends. In his study of sleep, Patrick McNamara, a neurobiologist, connects dreams with imaginative play, but from the night-world side of the relationship. For about twenty years, I had a fairly regular habit of sleepwalking. I was reading McNamara's book *An Evolutionary Psychology of Sleep and Dreams* for some clues about my getting out of bed in the middle of the night, walking over to the window looking for the parade that's coming through our backyard and getting upset because I'm supposed to be in it but I am too late. Unlike the many sleepwalkers who have to be told of their nighttime wanderings, I remember it all, not only what I was doing but what I was thinking.

Scouring the book didn't take me very far into my condition—except that sleepwalking runs in families and occurs during slow-wave sleep, the deepest stage, as do children's "night terrors." Missing a parade may seem far removed from a terror, but it would upset me all the same. The sleepwalking episodes seemed to come from nowhere, in my thirties, and without explanation disappeared. (Oddly enough, the last sleepwalking incident I've had in the last three years and counting was in the Dominican Republic, right before meeting Cristal. I don't know what to make of that still.) McNamara's book was far more helpful for me with its descriptions of the deep similarities between dreams and children's imaginative play. Both dreams and play involve simulations of the world for their own sake, with no obvious purpose, and are often accompanied by strong emotions. In addition, both dreams and imaginative play frequently display proteanism—that is, elements as wild, cagey, and unpredictable as an old sea god.

I discovered through this foray into sleep and dreams that the term *proteanism* has come to mean something very specific in the world of biology: unpredictability among animals. Unpredictability is critical to survival. How so? Although mercurial, erratic behaviors in our personal relationships and work places are generally unhelpful and threaten social stability, this is not what biologists are talking about. Instead, watch a rabbit run and you will get a better idea. Rabbits rarely run in a straight line. They act like they're heading one way, then shift, zig this way, zag back again until they find cover. They are like children in a game of tag, attempting to get away from the one who is "it," trying to reach base. And that is not far from what rabbits, or zebras, antelopes, deer, and so many prey species do. They have developed erratic, unpredictable escape patterns, ones that paradoxically are not patterns at all. From an evolutionary perspective, the rabbits that ran in predictable ways lost the race to the swifter fox or owl predators.

Erratic running is only one of many protean survival techniques. Ducklings, for example, travel along the water in clusters. But when any kind of audible or visual threat presents itself, the ducklings quickly dive under water, then scatter in unpredictable ways. The attention of a predator scatters as well, increasing the odds that most, if not all the ducklings, will survive. Fish that travel in schools display a similar scattering strategy. Other creatures, such as lizards and mice, will go into convulsions when threatened, flat-out confusing their attackers. Some types of moths will drop to the ground, motionless, but if they are then touched, they go wild, startling their enemy. And in one of the most fascinating and complex versions of proteanism, some birds, when protecting a nest, will feign injury. In the face of a threat, they may drop to the ground and hobble along as if they have a hurt leg (much like a "flopping" soccer player) or flap oddly as if a wing were injured, getting the attention of the predator. The flopping bird leads the threat away from the nest, but when it is about to get attacked itself, it resumes full faculties to get away.

Then again not all floppers, feigners, scatterers, and erratic runners get away. Otherwise, the predators would never have survived. Attackers, too, have developed forms of unpredictability to feed themselves and their young: the stealth of a bobcat that suddenly pounces, the speed of a cheetah that can catch prey before it gets a chance to zig or zag. Some creatures—weasels, for example—will exhibit crazy, convulsive-looking "dances" to grab the attention of a potential meal, then suddenly spring. Whether predator or prey, the larger point is that animal brains that produce only predictability do not survive.

In humans, proteanism shows up in everything from sports (surprising moves, unpredictable plays, faking one way and going another) to the arts (the plot twist of a novel, a new style of music, a startling combination of images in a poem or colors in a painting). The art of comedy, for example, depends upon surprise, juxtaposing ideas, words, or scenes in ways the audience doesn't see coming. Breakthroughs in science and technology come not only from carefully laid experimental plans for mice and men but from reimagining problems from a different angle, from intuitions, or even from solutions that spontaneously show up in showers and sleep, as if from nowhere.

This morning, as I shooed a fat rabbit from the fresh sprouts of my vegetable garden, I was impressed yet again by the odd escape route taken. Two short hops, a third in a different direction—slow. I don't seem to be a huge threat. It watches me, turns slightly. I clap. That did it. It dashes between me and the fence, and another bunny comes out of the garden and into the cover of a shrub. The original rabbit is out of sight now too. I realize how deep unpredictability must run in the rabbit soul if generation after generation inherits these pattern-bending patterns.So too in the human soul. Being unpredictable must be more than willpower, as if we could easily decide to become creative, willing ourselves into it: "I think I can, I think I can, I think I can be unpredictable, I think I can be creative." Most of the time, most of us think and act according to convention. Life together depends on it, from knowing the rules of the road and when school starts to understanding the value of money and where to buy food. Social life demands predictability. Simultaneously, the world throws circumstances our way that demand unconventional responses. The Mediterranean winds stall out and Meneláos and his starving sailors must find another way to survive—through divine inspiration, if only they can catch hold of the old shapeshifting god. Improvisation, creativity, innovation, ingenuity, and originality have served us well ever since our ancestors began chopping animal bones for marrow and sparking fires for protection. Neither conventionality nor unconventionality alone would get us very far down the survivability road.

But dreams and imaginary friendships hold the predictable and unpredictable together. I dream of holding my two-month-old granddaughter and she invents a language. Lucy is a mom and goes to work, yet can become a tiger. In a dream I walk through my house and discover a whole section I never knew was there. Jeff is good at karate and sometimes shifts into Jeffette who likes jewelry. My brother looks like last night's waiter. Coda dies from too big a bite, yet comes back to life. Ordinary scenes—simulations drawn from conventional reality—with a twist. Like magical realism in literature, dreams and imaginative play generate settings, characters, and plots that often resemble those in the everyday world but unpredictably transform them into protean scenes, sequences, and personalities, often laced with intense emotional engagement. Dreams and imaginative play are a kind of yoga for our souls, stretching the muscles of our predictable thoughts and ideas while engaging our hearts in the loves, losses, fears, and joys of life.

I think of a favorite book about dreams, one I reread frequently to loosen my grip on conventionality. *The Dream and the Underworld*, by renegade Jungian James Hillman, is full of protean twists and surprises reflective of the realm he explores. The challenge for those reflecting upon their own dream lives, as Hillman sees it, is not interpreting figures and events to fit into the daylight world of everyday categories and ways of thinking that some dream books offer—a car is your ego, food is knowledge. That's wronging a well. For Hillman, such an approach is to wrong the dream with our predictable minds. Instead, the dream world is a chance to enter a more dimly lit realm where our categories and interpretations are not so clear or where they may fall apart completely: "All sorts of what would be incompatibilities from the dayworld view exist side-by-side and easily convert one into another." Though Hillman is working from a very different perspective than that of a neurobiologist, there is a convergence with this underworld notion that our night selves may be generating protean possibilities in us. As our bodies relax in sleep, as our minds ease from the bright, hard-edged dayworld, new rooms appear in the mansion of our minds, spaces we didn't know existed and where anything can happen.

In play too. Over and over, we asked children, "What do you like to do with your friends nobody else can see?"

"Play." Though some children named other activities—reading together, doing homework, spelling, walking home—the overwhelming majority of them said they play. In pretend play, like dreams, the hard edges of realism are also relaxed. A popsicle stick becomes a comb, wooden blocks become a house, a child becomes a superhero who can fly, a toy tiger becomes the adventuring companion Hobbes. And it's fun. Not only does a child in play suspend a piece of conventional reality, but the suspension itself facilitates the play in some kind of infinite, self-reinforcing loop. Fun is the goal, if it can be called a goal, and fun is another way of saying there is no other purpose beyond the joy of playing itself. The same is true in play that is not particularly imaginative. Roll a ball to a toddler, she rolls it back. Repeat. Fun.

Even animals do it. Most primates and lots of mammals—typically creatures that care for their young—engage in one form of play or another, often wrestling or chasing, not so unlike kids on a preschool playground. Roughly, the longer the period of care in a species, the more likely and often the young will play. Why? Play requires a relaxed state, nearly impossible without a strong sense of security. Predators and threats are the responsibility of someone else: the adults. One school of thought is that in play the youth of a species are developing the skills and physiology needed in adulthood for survival—for example, fighting, hunting, or escaping. Play, here, is practice for the big show. And even bees, sharks, birds, and reptiles can exhibit play-like behavior, but frankly, with such creatures, it's hard to tell. Presumably playful wrestling or running is indeed helpful practice for serious fighting or escaping, but could there be more to it than such a functionalist view captures? After all, grown-ups play. Not only humans but adult zoo animals have been known to engage in playful behaviors: an aquatic turtle bangs a basketball around its tank; sharks chase a ball on a rope thrown by a zoo keeper. Perhaps they, like human children, have the luxury of not worrying about predators and therefore are more likely to play than those in the wild. Still, even wild animals play.

In a lecture on the subject (for an online TED Talk), play theorist Stuart Brown shows a remarkable sequence of photos in which a polar bear, in full predatory gaze, is about to attack a domesticated dog, a husky that is part of a sled team. The dog moves into a "play bow" and wags her tail, a behavior younger puppies will often exhibit with one another. "Something very unusual happens," Brown says of the bear. "That fixed behavior that is rigid and stereotyped and ends up with a meal—changes." The bear rises, stands over the husky, but with no fangs or claws extended. They begin "a play ballet"; they wrestle and roll around and fake bite one another. "They are in an altered state, they're in a state of play. And it's that state that allows these two creatures to explore the possible." Brown points to this as "a marvelous example of how a differential in power can be overridden by a process of nature that is within all of us." Did the dog go into a play state to trick the bear into not making a meal of her? Perhaps. No doubt that play here increased survivability in the most immediate manner. But it could be that the dog—a member of another highly social species in a pack of them—was not in the habit of genuine fighting. Maybe the dog had only ever play battled. We'll never know, but the incident illustrates how play—even pretend play—is not confined to the human world and how play can disrupt the relatively rigid conventional reality of predator and prey.

While play may be good practice for the grown-up show, I'm increasingly impressed by the protean possibilities it generates. Another school of thought about play emphasizes its creative function. Play offers opportunities to try out a wide variety of behaviors and strategies in a relatively safe way and with immediate, rather than delayed, benefits. Play helps one know the environment, especially when it is new or shifting. Horses set loose in new fields will run and play more than usual and by doing so, get to know their new surroundings. Mice that engage in locomotive play (voluntarily running on a wheel) show increased brain function. Parents' physical play with their infants correlates with lower levels of stress and emotional reactivity in the babies. With such immediate benefits, play is self-reinforcing, again, fun.

A lucky dog who just wants to have fun may live to play another day.

Both physical and social play enhance what is called *cognitive plasticity*: a readiness for learning, problem solving, skill development, and social facility. Such mental flexibility is particularly helpful for adapting to new situations or generating new possibilities in the midst of old ones. A species that plays a lot is able to adapt and improvise a lot. For the human species, this seems to have taken us to new vistas, allowing us to branch out into radically different environments around the globe, even to the US Midwest, where the weather is changing all the time!

The protean point is that play enhances the ability to be unpredictable and respond to surprising challenges. If the wildness of our dreams loosens our grip on conventional ways, likewise play—from the wild world of imaginary friends to tossing a ball around—may loosen us from rigid ways of thinking and behaving and prepare us for the unexpected. Perhaps this is why sports and playground games offer such vivid examples of protean behavior: a game of tag with zigzagging children, a fake pass of the basketball one way followed by a throw the other, or a surprise strategy by a soccer team, a play nobody has seen before. Playgrounds and games provide the setting—the protection, in a sense—within which play can happen and protean moves can be executed and responded to. Play provides the chance to practice both skill and surprise.

After receiving instructions from the sea-nymph, Meneláos takes three brave lads and they hide in a cave where Proteus takes his noon nap. They grab him, but, as his daughter predicted, the shapeshifting god resists, taking on "a whiskered lion's shape, a serpent then; a leopard; a great boar; then sousing water; then a tall green tree." But the sailors hang on tight until Proteus gives up and listens to their woes. He explains the proper sacrifice needed by Zeus to set things right and deliver the wind needed to sail on.

Wild mind: shapeshifters, dreams, raccoons transforming into skunks, fake fighting across species, rabbits' erratic running, and cognitive plasticity. What a paradox, I realize. As night dreams and imaginative play relax our grip on the hard-edged dayworld, we are better prepared for it: to face the unexpected, explore, learn, problem solve, improvise, understand, adapt, and more. But the greatest paradox our cognition presents is this: we can recognize an abiding essence in the midst of change, one that cuts through categories and kinds to see the heart of another, a sacred reflection—if we can hold on.

A fascinating, if not theological, footnote to Sophia and her shape-shifting Lucy is provided by Sophia's mother. As a practicing Catholic, Mom explained that she had taught Sophia "that God was her best friend" and "that God can change forms, being whatever you need God to be." She then added, "which is what Lucy does." Sophia's mother, who'd had an invisible friend herself as a little girl, was happy to welcome Lucy to the family. She was also happy to welcome the analogy with religious belief.

PART II
Away

CHAPTER 6

WHO KNOWS WHAT?

"I see nobody on the road," said Alice.
"I only wish I had such eyes," the King remarked
in a fretful tone. "To be able to see Nobody!"

"THIS IS FASCINATING," I said to Jane. "It's theory of mind—again!"

Jane was driving. We were on the stretch of Interstate 71 between Columbus, Ohio, and Cleveland, on our way to pick up Cora and David from the College of Wooster. Cora had just finished her first year; David was graduating the next day. I was reading Marjorie Taylor's *Imaginary Companions and the Children Who Create Them,* in a section of the book called "Theory of Mind."

"Okay?" Jane responded, waiting for more.

I read a sentence from the book, with emphasis, "We found that children who *had* imaginary companions did better on the theory of mind tasks than the other children."

"That's interesting—I guess," she commented. "But what's theory of mind?"

"Essentially," I said, "it's understanding the mind of someone else—what we think they know or don't know."

"Mind reading," she concluded, and she was right.

This was only a few months after our Yucatán trip (where the idea of studying IFs had reemerged). I was in a reading phase of research, and it would be another year before I'd actually interview any children. I was familiar with theory-of-mind research from the cognitive psychologist Justin Barrett, whose work I discovered in a *New York Times* article and had just presented to a class. When I read the section from Taylor's book, I had a hunch it would help, but at that point, I was not entirely clear how.

⁕⁕⁕

Theory of mind is shorthand for the ways we attribute beliefs, knowledge, desires, intentions—in short, a mind—to others. It's called a *theory* because minds are more or less invisible. Even babies sense an agency behind your adoring eyes and warm arms, unseen intentions directing your behavior. This is no more conscious on their part than breathing or crying; they just know.

But the mind is complicated. Syllogisms pale compared to understanding the weird, complex universe behind our behavior. Not the least, the invisibility of the mind blankets our intuitive abilities with ambiguities, doubts, and haze. A simple example: children have to learn that minds can be wrong. I ask three-year-old Cora to fetch David from the basement for dinner. He's not there; he's in the living room reading. She'll have to fine-tune her theory of my mind to include the possibility that minds can have bad information. It won't be the last time. One theory about why children pretend at all is that they are playing in this theory of mind, stuff more malleable than a can of Play-Doh. They are like horses running around new fields, learning and discovering about this invisible territory of human minds.

"If I showed this box to your Mom, what would she think is inside it?" To investigate this fine-tuning of the developing theory of mind, Barrett showed children that a cracker box actually contained rocks instead of the saltines pictured on the outside—a *surprising-contents* test. When he asked the children what a parent would think is inside the box, children under five or six would say, "Rocks." Older children answered, "Crackers." Six-year-olds understood that someone looking at the box would be fooled, would have a false belief about the contents. But younger children assume others know.

Decades earlier, Piaget had found similar results in his perspective-taking experiments. Young children were not good at distinguishing their own point of view from that of others. Ask a four-year-old, as he did, what a doll on the other side of a mountain display sees, she'll say the doll sees what the child sees. For Piaget, this was more proof of early childhood egocentrism. Young children are locked into their own worlds so much that they don't realize other people might have another, different perspective. That was Piaget's theory of kids' minds.

But here was Marjorie Taylor saying that children with imaginary friends performed better on a series of theory-of-mind tests. For example, in one of them she showed four-year-olds that a raisin box actually contained a toy. The children with imaginary companions were more likely than children without them to say that a puppet would be fooled and think raisins were inside the box. From Piaget's view of children's egocentrism, this makes no sense. How could kids who are so full of "ludistic tendencies," as he put it, that they cannot differentiate fantasy friendships from the visible kind be better at understanding the subtleties of who knows what? But from another point of view, one more generous to the imagination and invisible friends, the finding makes great sense. Children with imaginary friends are practicing points of view all the time: "Crystal would like a cookie too." "That crayon sure is curious." Or even "Paw-Paw comes to make me feel better." Appreciating the knowledge, desires, intentions, or perspectives of others is ultimately an act of the imagination. By playing with mind, by imaginatively representing other minds—even when invisible—children are fine-tuning their ability to understand others. "And it's kind of fun!"

As we moved out of the flatland of central Ohio and into the rolling hills of the north, I explained the research to Jane. She said, "So Crystal made Cora a better mind reader." We both pondered that thought for a while. It's hard to know what comes first. Maybe good mind readers, kids who are socially attuned, are more apt to have invisible friends. Or having imaginary friends sharpens our ability to understand other minds.

We came to our turnoff, Highway 30. Jane broke the silence, "So what would Crystal think is in the box?" We both laughed. A year later, an invitation came that sharpened the focus of the research and led me to pose this exact question.

⌇⌇⌇⌇⌇⌇⌇⌇⌇⌇⌇⌇

The email was forwarded from a friend. *The Cognition, Religion, and Theology Project (University of Oxford) is hosting a Summer Workshop on the cognitive science of religion. The workshop will provide scholars who are interested in conducting empirical research in the area, but who have little or no experience in quantitative methods, with training in relevant techniques and tools (e.g., measurement, quantitative analysis, experimental design).*

Summer came and I found myself landing in London's Heathrow and soon on a bus out to Oxford for, as Jane called it, "nerd camp."

The next morning, still jet-lagged, I was one of the last to arrive for our first meeting. I'd had trouble finding the Dodgson Room in the collection of buildings that seemed to move around on me. Christ Church is one of thirty-eight colleges composing the University of Oxford. Though the university dates to the twelfth century, Christ Church is younger, founded in the sixteenth century by King Henry VIII, whose portrait hangs front and center in the Great Hall, surrounded by portraits of the college's famous alumni—from John and Charles Wesley to John Locke and William Penn. But more impressive to my family was the fact that several scenes in the Harry Potter films were shot on the grounds of the college, and the Great Hall was itself the model for the magnificent dining hall in the movies. There were about thirty of us, from all parts of the world, participating in this Cognition, Religion, and Theology Project, an initiative of Oxford's Institute of Cognitive and Evolutionary Psychology.

The director of the event, Justin Barrett, was introducing the philosophy behind the effort. The project considered itself to be part of a relatively new discipline. As preparation, we had all been assigned readings in the field, including an overview by Barrett, published in 2007. "Fifteen years ago," the piece begins, "there was no such thing as cognitive science of religion. Only a handful of scholars independently using insights from the cognitive sciences to study religion existed." Some of those scholars were in the room—anthropologists, cognitive and experimental psychologists, theologians, and philosophers, attesting to the diversity of disciplines coming together around this new field. Many practiced one religion or another; many did not.

What makes Barrett's own research not only cognitive psychology or cognitive science but *cognitive science of religion* is his exploration of the way minds intersect with religious stuff, the beliefs and practices that characterize religions around the world. For example, in his theory-of-mind studies, he asked children not only what a puppet or parent would think is in a cracker box, but he asked them what God would think. By five or six years, kids understand that a person will have a false belief and think crackers are in the box. But these same youngsters said God would know rocks are actually in the box. That was stunning. The assumption had been that children this age think of God in very concrete terms, as a big person in the sky, and do so until later childhood, maybe until eight or nine, when they can begin to imagine a point of view large enough to know everything. But if children are basing God's mind on human minds, why does God know rocks are in the box? When children learn that people can have false beliefs, they should think God can too. Much as younger children can solve syllogisms under the right conditions, Barrett discovered they can differentiate who knows what at much younger ages, including what God knows verses ordinary mortals.

"Children, especially young children," Barrett was offering the room, "easily learn natural languages, anywhere around the world. But they do not easily learn binary code." Having read his book *Why Would Anyone Believe in God?*, I was familiar with the idea. But his statement focused the argument for me. The notion is that the mind—cognition—constrains or channels the types of language humans create and understand. Computers work well with binary code, but human beings are not cognitively prepared to easily understand that 01110100 01101000 01100101 00100000 01100011 01100001 01110100 00100000 01101001 01101110 00100000 01110100 01101000 01100101 00100000 01101000 01100001 01110100 means "the cat in the hat." "In a similar way," Barrett continued, "our minds may affect religious beliefs and expressions." Some beliefs and practices may come more easily to the human mind than others, may be more easily transmitted to others, and the tools of cognitive science may help us better understand what those are and why.

The idea that God could know in extraordinary ways—know that rocks are in the box—may be one of those beliefs that comes easily to the human mind. Believing that some—not only God but angels, spirits, ancestors, prophets, mediums, gurus, and more—have special knowledge may be a very human mental tendency. For Barrett, the fact that very young children think others—not only parents and God but bears and ants even—will think rocks are in the box may give such beliefs a running start. Children have to learn that people have false beliefs, which means undoing the assumption that they know. With God or other special beings, nothing has to be undone.

As I sat in the Dodgson Room listening to Barrett describe the tools of cognitive science, I was struck by the paradox. Empirical methods, those tools devoted to scientific observation, could be employed to investigate something invisible. Not only gods and imaginary friends but invisible minds. Some in this emerging field find such research an opportunity to liberate us from the biases of minds bent on finding meaning and gods around every corner. The hope is similar to Freud's in a way, though the mechanics are different. By explaining how we're primed to believe, even though it's all an illusion, we can explain away religion. Others, including the speaker, point out how unscientific such a conclusion is and adopt a humbler stance towards a world and a mind that is infinitely complex. In this view, cognitive science of religion helps us explore one area of such complexity. "Suppose science produces a convincing account for why I think my wife loves me," Barrett asked the *New York Times* interviewer, "should I then stop believing that she does?"

The Cognition, Religion, and Theology Project—I think of it as the Harry Potter Project—was divided into two groups: one "philosophical," the other "empirical," with about a dozen in each group who were a mix of new and established scholars. My theological training made me a much better fit for the philosophical group, but those of us in the empirical group would have the chance to develop an actual study, with people. The next thing I knew I was sitting in front of a laptop practicing *t*-tests and regression analyses using Excel spreadsheets. I seriously questioned whether I was in the right group. I'd had stats and research methods as part of my graduate program, but that had been twenty years earlier. I had never even used Excel before and between the numbers, software, and jet lag, I was on the edge of freaking out. We broke for lunch just in time.

In the Hogwarts dining hall, I noticed a portrait of the conference room's namesake, Charles Dodgson. I stared at him, wondering who he was and how I'd gotten myself into this mathematical mess. He offered no clues, except a relaxed look on his face. "Get a grip," I told myself, or maybe it was the portrait talking. Everyone else in the group was in the same empirical boat. The whole idea was to train those with little working experience with scientific methods of study—scholars from religious studies, philosophy, theology, or the humanities—to learn disciplined methods of empirical research. I sat for lunch and I could feel my pulse slow down.

I thought about a wonderful book I had read by a British writer named Adam Zeman. The book has the clever title *Consciousness: A User's Guide.* Zeman had been trained in philosophy before turning to medicine. He uses an analogy from language to lay out the dilemma of trying to study the mind with scientific methods. There is an irreducible tension between first-person experience and third-person description. The third-person objectivity that science strives for is public, repeatable, impersonal, and it tries to eliminate first-person subjectivity. Yet, as Zeman affirms, first-person, private, unique, personal experience matters intensely and is why medical issues such as epilepsy or Alzheimer's can make life so difficult.

An empirical group and a philosophical group. Were we replicating this great divide between personal and public?

In the afternoon, Barrett asked each of us to share our research interests and initial idea for a study. My empirical-group mates shared some wonderful ideas for exploring cognition in the midst of a wide variety of cultures—Shinto Japan, Sikh India, Confucian China, New Age California, highly educated England, and more. I was impressed and intimidated. My turn. "Believe it or not," I said, sweating, "I'd like to study imaginary friends." Everyone waited politely. "I'd like to work on two fronts. One, collect stories. Two, well, theory of mind." I searched for the most succinct way to put it. "I'm wondering what an imaginary friend thinks is in the box."

Barrett nodded his head and simply offered, "Interesting." It seemed close enough to an affirmation to keep me going.

Before dinner, seven or eight of us decided to go for a run around Oxford. Barrett is a former cross-country runner and offered to lead the way. "Why are so many of us runners?" I wondered as I tried to keep up with the younger athletes—"good runners!" We were given a fast but marvelous tour through the city and countryside surrounding the historic village. Such a culturally and historically rich place full of museums, famous colleges, pubs where writers like J. R. R. Tolkien and C. S. Lewis hung out. I was especially excited to see the university track, for my dad's sake; he had been a coach and runner. While Dad was racing the mile in college, Roger Bannister broke the four-minute barrier—and had done so on the Oxford track.

About a half hour into our run, we approached the edge of a field, and someone pointed to a church. "I hear the well's over there." One of the guys explained that it was the well from Alice in Wonderland. Frankly, I didn't remember a well in the story (I later found out the Dormouse described a "treacle well" during the tea party with the Mad Hatter).

I asked, "Lewis Carroll lived here?"

He had, another runner explained, and not only that, he had taught at Christ Church College (Hogwarts). In addition to writing books for children, he taught math and logic at the college. "But his real name was Charles Dodgson."

The next afternoon we were treated to a fascinating example of the kind of research that used empirical methods to explore religious stuff. When I first saw Richard Sosis, a tall, trim, heavily bearded anthropologist, he reminded me of a young Jerry Garcia of the Grateful Dead band. Sosis studies the interaction of religion and cooperation. A genial sort, he was nonetheless decidedly uncooperative on one matter. For dinner in Hogwarts, the men of our group were asked to wear ties, but he refused.

Without further information, he said he'd given them up. "But I like that one," he offered, referring to a purple number I was wearing. I turned it around so that he could see the label: Jerry Garcia. The design was based upon one of the singer's paintings. Like running, it was uncanny how many of us were fans of Garcia and the Dead, and long musical discussions ensued.

Beyond discussing music and helping us with research methods, Sosis presented an analysis he had conducted of nineteenth-century US communes. He discovered that religious communes endured longer than nonreligious ones, and his hunch was that religious communes co-operated more, which enhanced community longevity. Later, in a study among kibbutzim in Israel, he compared religious communes to secular ones using a simple game, one rooted in economic theory. Members of the same kibbutz are partnered but don't know with whom. Each is shown an envelope with 100 shekels inside. (A shekel is worth about one US quarter.) Each partner can take as many of the 100 as they like and keep them, but only if the sum of both does not exceed 100. The tricky thing is that whatever remains in the envelope is increased by 50 percent and split evenly between the two people. The best team decision is to choose zero, leaving 100 shekels and making the total payout 150 shekels (75 each). But guessing your partner might choose zero, you could greedily take advantage and choose 100, for even more, leaving your partner with nothing.

The results: members of religious kibbutzim were significantly more cooperative with each other than members of the secular kibbutzim (who pocketed more money overall). It seems religion may intensify communal concern. That's the good news of religion, at least for in-group cooperation. The backside is that in-group cooperation can occur at the expense of outsiders. Religion apparently has its own version of an angel sitting on one shoulder with a devil on the other. The good angel opens our hearts and imaginations to consider the needs and outlook of others, whether in our group or not. The devil tempts us to stick to our own kind.

The point of the presentation was to demonstrate empirically based methods to investigate religious minds and hearts.

Over the next two weeks, we spent mornings immersed in statistics and research methods, our afternoons developing research projects, and evenings soaking in Oxford, including its rich pub life. If all went well, we would each be eligible for a modest grant to facilitate our research. I proposed a project about imaginary friends with two components: one, stories gathered from interviews with children about these special friends, exploring their relationship with the invisible; and two, theory-of-mind tests with each child, asking them what others know, including their imaginary friend and God. I wondered whether invisible friends would be more like an ordinary mortal or more like God.

We would find out whether we got funding for our projects in a couple of weeks, after returning home.

On the plane ride back to the US, I remembered a dream I'd had earlier in the summer, before England. I'm at a theater to see a play, in the lobby with friends, but when I go to my seat, I'm by myself. I'm sitting in the mezzanine, farther back than I would have liked, but I can see fine. There are a lot of kids in the opening scene of the play. They are playing with a ball. The ball flies into the audience. Someone tries to give it back. Then I notice a child whose face has been painted bright yellow, made up for the play. I recall that I saw him before the play began. He had come to the theater with his face already made up.

Pondering the dream, I tried to recall whether the ball ever made it back to the stage, but I couldn't remember. Nor could I recall any more about the child with the painted face. But it struck me that I had just visited the land of Shakespeare and the London stage, in the city of fantasy writers like Carroll, Tolkien, and Lewis, in a school of philosophers and theologians like Locke and the Wesley brothers, in the dining hall of Hogwarts, thinking about the made-up worlds of children. I thought, "I'm through the looking glass now."

By the time fall classes started, I'd gotten the go-ahead from Oxford for the project and soon had a research team together and started interviewing, beginning with Nicole and her two friends Leah and Coda. After interviewing each of the children you've encountered here already about their invisible friends, we conducted theory-of-mind tests with them.

Inspired by a road trip to Ohio and by nerd camp in Oxford, I finally got to ask, "What would Crystal think is in the box?"

Barrett and the empirical gang thought it would be helpful to conduct more than one theory-of-mind test in case the type of test mattered. Plus multiple tests would generate more data. Thinking about the attention and patience of preschoolers, I knew they needed to be simple enough to finish quickly, and I landed on three different tasks. The first is called an *occluded-picture* task. We showed each child a green file folder and said that there was a picture inside, part of which was visible through a small window cut into the front of the folder. After explaining that only part of a bigger picture was visible, we asked whether the child knew what the whole picture was. Most of the children, regardless of age, guessed: for example, "a man watching TV" or "someone on a computer," but, as they would soon find out, they were wrong. Each child was then asked about four different figures (the psychological literature calls them *agents*): a good friend (the visible kind), their invisible friend, a dog, and God. Would these agents know what the whole picture is if nobody showed them the inside of the folder? Then we opened the folder to reveal the whole picture.

Occluded Picture (before)

Most of the children were tickled by the picture, "Oh, an elephant on a ball!" We closed the folder and asked the exact same question again for each agent. The only difference was that now the child had seen the whole picture. Children with a well-developed theory of mind should now say that their best friend or a dog would *not* know what the whole picture is. These children would understand that the partial view through the window does not provide enough information to identify the picture as an elephant on a ball, at least for ordinary types of minds.

In a second task, a *background-knowledge* test, we showed children three different scribbles, each on its own full sheet of paper. We told the children that the scribbles "are part of a secret code I made up and have not taught to anyone else, and each scribble stands for something, but no one else knows what they mean." After asking whether they and the others knew what the scribbles meant (again they often guessed), we taught them the meaning of each (tree, book, sun). I still chuckle thinking about the creation of this test. When I first tried out the scribbles with the research team, I had trouble remembering which scribble meant what. I finally made the tree scribble green, the book black, and the sun yellow to help me remember. While this scribble test is similar to the elephant-on-a-ball occluded-picture task, it is slightly different as it explores the role of background knowledge—the code—in the ways children think about other minds. It is less about seeing and more about information.

The final test was quick. At this point, children can easily begin to weary of the questions, though stickers after each round help. If nothing else in the research, I learned how much kids love stickers! This last task was an actual *false-belief* test, similar to the cracker-box test of Barrett. We showed children a crayon box and asked whether they knew the contents. All the children did, or at least thought they did, before they were shown that the box actually contained small rocks. We put the rocks

Occluded Picture (after)

back in the box and asked what each agent would think was in the box on seeing it for the first time.

There were some slight variations in the response patterns between the tests, but, using my newly won skills of analysis (as well as finding an experienced statistician to check my work), none of the differences between tests was statistically significant. Whether the tests were considered separately or together, the basic developmental pattern was the same. Younger children tended to think everyone, from the dog to God, would know whatever there was to know—the whole picture, the meaning of the scribbles, or that rocks were in the box. Older children were able to appreciate the limits of human and doggie minds. To my surprise, however, one older child said a dog would indeed know rocks were in the box, even though she said the dog would not know the whole picture or scribble code. When the test was over, I asked her how the dog would know. She said, "The dog would sniff and be able to smell the rocks inside." She outsmarted the test.

Children of all ages overwhelmingly thought God would know whatever there was to know, and over half of them (62 percent) said that their invisible friends would know. In other words, imaginary friends were "in between." They were more likely to know than a dog or a human but less likely to know than God. True to Barrett's research, the study does seem to show how ready, prepared, and primed children are to attribute special powers of knowing to some types of agents. In other theory-of-mind studies, children are told that a figure has special powers (for example, "Mr. Smart knows everything"; "this cat can see in the dark"), and children easily adjust their responses accordingly, suggesting how natural attributing special powers to some agents is for children.

What most impressed me was how many children spontaneously attributed special knowing abilities to their imaginary friends. Nearly all the children came from households that practiced religion at some level—going to Sunday school or worship or praying at meals or bedtime, for example. Their understandings of God are bolstered by religious education, practice, and the culture in general (even the children not involved in religion knew about God). But not so much for imaginary friends. They are not generally the subjects of education or general cultural messages such as "Crystal knows what's in your heart" or "Quack-Quack knows everything" or "Leah sees all."

Children can be taught to think about what God's special powers are; they can be taught that cats see in the dark or that dogs can smell through boxes; but children make up their own rules about the powers of their invisible friends. Perhaps their invisibility itself is important. The physicality of humans and dogs is what creates limits in perspectives and knowledge, at least the older children might reason. Perhaps invisible figures enjoy the privileges of not being so limited because they don't have ordinary bodies. Regardless, so many children spontaneously attributing special knowing abilities to their invisible friends—even when they understand false belief—suggests a deep bias in our theory of mind, one that makes beliefs about God's mind easy to affirm and pass along.

After my year of interviewing children in Louisville, the Harry Potter gang was back in Oxford presenting our findings to one another and discussing the implications. I had just presented mine and it was well received, both the stories of Quack-Quack and other friends as well as the results of the cognitive tests. But several from this heavily international crew had the same question: What about children in other cultures? "I have the same question, but can't answer that," I said, "not based on a few dozen children in one corner of Kentucky." The closest relative to our invisible friend study was one conducted by Nicola Knight among Mayan children in the Yucatán of Mexico. He created a false-belief test by placing a pair of shorts in a container that would normally have tortillas inside, much like rocks being in a crayon or cracker box. He did not ask about imaginary friends, but he did ask children about some other intriguing characters. In addition to more ordinary creatures—jaguar, bee, dog, human—he also asked children about God (the Roman Catholic God of the surrounding culture), the Sun (a traditional member of the Mayan pantheon), as well as mischievous elf-like forest spirits called the *arux*. These kids thought the arux and Sun were more likely than humans or animals to know shorts were in the container, but less likely than God. Like imaginary friends, they were *in-betweens*.

As I reflected on this pattern, I found myself thinking about the way so many cultures and religions around the planet have something like in-betweens, figures moving between worlds like angels on Jacob's ladder. Not only angels and arux, but ghosts, spirits, ancestors, jinn, and so many more. It's as if the human mind bends toward "seeing" a world teeming with invisibles.

Home from Oxford, I was in between. The research was over; the Cognition, Religion, and Theology Project was concluding and had no more grants to give, not even small ones. Yet I felt I had just begun. My next move would get clearer over a dinner conversation.

Jane and I were having a meal with friends, Christy and Bruce, and their new baby. Jane had conducted their wedding a couple years earlier, and now Cora was working at Bruce's restaurant. They had us over for a meal, a treat since Bruce is a top-of-the-line fine-dining chef. His restaurant specializes in Mayan food because he is from the Yucatán. Jane mentioned I'd recently been to England, and one thread led to another and soon we were talking about imaginary friends. I still had cross-cultural questions in mind, left over from the Oxford presentation, wondering not only if kids would answer similarly on theory-of-mind tasks but whether kids in other, very different cultures from the US even had invisible friends. All the studies I knew took place in the US, Europe, or Australia.

I asked Bruce whether he had had an invisible friend as a child and whether he thought kids where he grew up had them. "The *alux*!" he said immediately. "They were all over. Usually you can't see them, but some people do." While a variation on the theme of invisible friends, I wanted to hear more. He explained that the alux are little spirits that run around in the fields and forests. "They might help you, but they might play tricks on you." I realized as he spoke he was talking about the same spirits that Knight had studied—alux and arux. Apparently the Knight translators heard an *r* for this Mayan dialect's *l* sound, which illustrates how tricky this cross-cultural enterprise can be. "You've got to go study the alux," he said.

"Yes," I said, excited, "I'd love to."

I realized that even though the Oxford project was wrapping up, the organization that funded it, the John Templeton Foundation, might be interested. They specialize in research that puts religion and science in conversation. I got in touch; they welcomed a proposal; and a year later, I was initiating a cross-cultural version of the original IF Project.

As I write about it now, I can say that I've been to some captivating places since, but I still have not had the opportunity to study the alux. I hope to one day. As I think back over the last decade, I wonder though whether the alux have been studying me. Maybe ten years ago some mischievous Mayan elf instigated this wild ride of research I've been on to see what would happen—an empirical test of my theory of mind. Maybe an alux snuck on that bus to Valladolid, popped in the DVD of *Millions*, surrounded me with scads of alux friends among the ruins of Chichén Itzá, and moved me to write down the letters *IF* in a notebook. I've been playing tricks on kids since, filling crayon boxes with rocks, making up secret codes, showing partial pictures. Maybe these tricksters wanted to see whether I would know what the whole picture is.

CHAPTER 7

ANCESTORS AND ANGELS

*"Who in the world am I? Ah, that's
the great puzzle."*

HWAN, a boy six years old and full of sparkle, is running around the room; then he starts the camera rolling for his own interview. Hwan's mother, a native of Korea, explains that he is always talking to someone while he plays, even though nobody is there. A mutual friend told her about the study and she thought we might like to talk with Hwan.

"Do you know why you're here today?" Katrina asks the boy.

"So I can be the cameraman?"

"So you can be the cameraman!" Katrina laughs. "No, I want to talk to you about some of your friends."

Anticipating where this was going Hwan responds, "Well, the invisible friend, Holy Spirit?"

Katrina, who had interviewed over a dozen children for the project at this point, freezes. She takes a deep breath, nods, and says "All right." Then silence.

After a few more seconds Hwan offers, "You can continue."

Hwan was never clear about who he was talking to in play, whether the Holy Spirit, another invisible friend, or himself. But he did explain that the Holy Spirit had arrived the previous Christmas and that they liked to read the Bible together and pray. When asked to illustrate his friend, Hwan drew a flame, a traditional Christian symbol for the Spirit taken from the biblical story of Pentecost in the book of Acts. Tongues of fire appeared and rested upon a gathering of followers of Jesus, and they were filled with the Holy Spirit, the Scripture says, and began to speak in other languages. The story itself plays on an even older one: the Tower of Babel from the book of Genesis, which tells how the one language of people became many. On Pentecost, the many languages of the world are spoken, but everyone hears their own native tongue and understands. For Hwan, who hears Korean at home and in church and uses English at school and among his friends, I can imagine how the juxtaposition of tongues and language with fire and Spirit must make for an intriguing story. Why not become friends with this Holy Spirit?

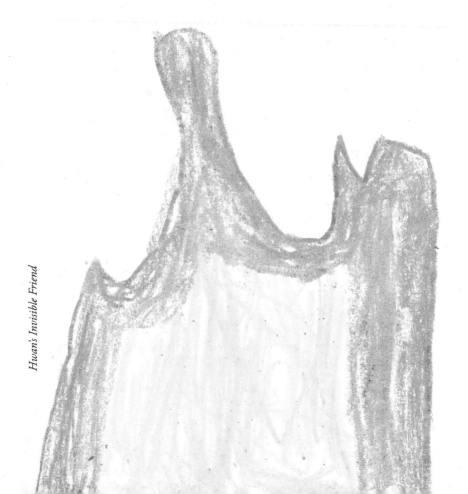

Hwan's Invisible Friend

I felt as if Hwan were looking over my shoulder as I drafted and redrafted interview questions I would pose to children in this cross-cultural phase of research. I was soon headed for East Africa, to Kenya, where my son, David, and daughter-in-law, Amy, were working. I would go from there to Malawi, where a friend lives. This was a chance to compare children's minds and imaginations across cultures. While the children in the Louisville study came from a variety of church denominations, nearly all were Christian. And with the exception of Hwan and two African American girls, the children were white Euro-Americans. A rich opportunity lay ahead. But time with children would be much more limited than it had been in the US, my questions and their answers would have to be translated, and I wasn't sure of the best way to ask about imaginary friends in places where they may not even have them.

Perhaps IFs are a feature of places with lots of resources for children, of cultures that emphasize play and recreation, especially in childhood. David had warned me that a colleague there had told him, "Children in Kenya don't have imaginary friends." He wasn't sure what that was based upon. The colleague who said this was from the US, had married a Kenyan man, and lived in the city. David's theory of mind knew she might be working with a false belief on the matter. "But your Dad should ask about the ancestors," she suggested, still encouraging the research. "They're everywhere and very important." She went on to say that they did not name their children for days after birth, not until an ancestor came in a dream to tell them what their names were.

Kenya is not unusual in this regard. Nearly every culture around the globe features invisible figures of one sort or another, from ghosts to gods. I thought if I found out Kenyan kids indeed do not have imaginary friends, that would be important information. And I could at least explore how children think about the minds of other types of invisible beings. For example, would the children tend to think ancestors know what ordinary mortals do not, much as the alux and the Sun did in the Mayan study? Whether or not children in Kenya or Malawi or other parts of the world have imaginary friends, I could still explore how they think about invisible minds.

So I was thinking about Hwan as I struggled to draft an interview protocol. He reminded me that the lines between an invisible friend and a religious figure are not always so clear. And once again the language we used to explore these questions would matter. To call the Holy Spirit an *imaginary* friend could be insulting to Hwan and his religious sensibilities, and I did not want to make the equivalent insult in another culture. *Invisible* friend, okay, but *imaginary* or *pretend* implies not real. Such a distinction was something the social scientist Antonia Mills discovered when she tried to determine whether children in India had "imaginary playmates," as she called them. She asked a gathering of psychologists as well as parents and people more generally whether they knew of any children with imaginary playmates, and "the answer was universally, 'no.' The common explanation was that children were never alone and therefore had no need to invent an imaginary companion." However, she eventually discovered children who did talk to figures that nobody else could see, and she determined that the issue was the term *imaginary*. These companions of children were believed to be beings from the spirit realm and/or from a previous life—real, not "imaginary." They were simply invisible. So how to avoid the same mistake if possible? How to respect the cultural differences and make meaningful comparisons to the culture from which I come?

Beneath these questions were ancient philosophical paradoxes about the One and the Many, the Universal and the Particular. To study anything about human existence is to entertain these puzzles. How much of childhood—whether play, imaginary friends, or theory-of-mind development—is cultural, rooted in the social patterns of a particular time and place? How much is universal, rooted in the kinds of bodies and brains we are born with? Consider language. Children around the world generally begin to babble by eight months of age, making repetitive *ba-ba-ba* and *ga-ga-ga* noises, playing with sounds and their ability to create them. On a continuum from universal to cultural phenomena, babbling skews heavily towards the universal. However, during that second year of life, those babbling sounds begin to take cultural shape, becoming words in English or Swahili, for example. Yet nothing is simple. Even before they babble, by six months of age babies around the globe can differentiate the language of their home from other languages, favoring the one they normally hear. Then again, some children never speak. In severe autism, for instance, children may never learn to use any language because of the difficulty of engaging the social-cultural world. Humans are generally deeply cultural beings, yet to be deeply cultural demands capacities such as sharing attention, hearing, and the production of sounds that seem to transcend any particular culture, capacities that run deep in our species.

In the weeks ahead, I was about to hike a path where the cultural and universal meet, making even the simplest questions of childhood development complicated. Invisible friends and mind reading could be more like shared attention and babbling or they could be more like Swahili. Add to this trek the vast individual differences between people within relatively homogenous cultures. Some children in the same family have imaginary friends, others don't; and some siblings share such a friend. Some imaginary friends are as shapeshifting as Proteus, others maintain stable shape. And so on.

The pressing pragmatic question remained: What do I ask children?

I finally landed on this approach: "Some children have friends that nobody else can see. Do you have any friends nobody else can see?" It is not a perfect question. It would miss the Winnie-the-Pooh or Calvin and Hobbes breed of imaginary friends rooted in a visible toy or doll. But it would bypass the imaginary-versus-real tension that Mills discovered in India and we found with Hwan's friend the Holy Spirit.

Soon I would be posing the question to children in a small Luo village within sight of Lake Victoria, or Nam Lolwe in the Luo language. The Luo are only one of dozens of ethnic groups that compose what is now the nation of Kenya. But the Luo are also in neighboring countries, mostly around Lake Victoria (in Uganda and Tanzania, for example), having settled in the region about the time Columbus sailed to the Americas. In recent years, they have become best known as the ethnic group of Barack Obama Senior, the US president's father. David and Amy were teaching in an Anglican school serving some of the poorest children in the region. Because of their teaching, they knew the families and children of the area well and could arrange interviews.

Before the interviews began, I had the opportunity to spend time with an expert in Luo culture, Professor Denis Oluoch-Oduor, who was teaching at a Catholic university outside Nairobi at the time and is Luo from the region near the city of Kisumu. A scholar of both Christian theology and Luo religion, he was able to introduce me to traditional Luo beliefs and practices as well as contemporary ones. He helped me identify other potential invisible figures that children would readily know about, in addition to God and possible imaginary friends. When I asked whether children had invisible friends, I did not get a clear answer. He, like David's colleague, began talking about ancestors. The ancestors—that is, the spirits of family members who have died—are indeed important figures in the lives of the Luo, he confirmed. They are buried on the family homestead and are considered to be present and involved in the everyday affairs of the living. They are allies to the family, frequenting dreams to provide wisdom when they are honored. But they can cause trouble for those who would dishonor them or the homestead. The professor provided more context for the ancestors by describing the traditional Luo understanding of the cosmos, the world seen and unseen. Three spheres compose the world: an upper, or sky, region (where God lives); the middle sphere of the living ("where we are," he said); and the underworld populated by the "living dead" (ancestors both recent and ancient). The spheres are interrelated, something those of us in the middle sphere may experience especially through dreams, in rituals, in prayer, and in the larger environment where trees and rain are so important. "When it rains, the underworld people are cooking," and when the ancestors have not been cooking enough to sustain crops and wells, people traditionally pray to the ancestors and offer libations to encourage rain.

When he told me this, I wondered for a moment how many prayers for rain have been offered through time and space on this planet. On the continuum between religious universal and particular, I imagine praying for rain must fall as near to the universal end as anything. And yet in Kenya, as in many parts of the world, even when the prayers are success-ful, holding onto the water has become increasingly difficult. Wangari Maathai, Kenyan and winner of the Noble Peace Prize for her environ-mental Green Belt Movement, has helped make her home country, if not the world, aware of the importance of trees to this middle sphere of life. When the forests are diminished for construction and development, the land loses its ability to hold water and its fertile topsoil washes away. Maathai initiated a tree-planting movement in Kenya; its first seven trees in downtown Nairobi in 1975 have turned into over 50 million and counting. Based upon traditional religious beliefs she learned as a child, she sees the environment as sacred, the hand of God stretching towards us to help us live. We slap that hand away at our own peril. If modern world views have made traditional reverence for the spirits in trees and rocks and streams difficult, they have come at high costs.

As Dr. Oluoch-Oduor was sharing with me the importance of the natural world in traditional Luo religion, he described a ritual in which the Sun is prayed to in the morning, addressed as "the eye of God." This caught my ear. The study by Nicola Knight among the Mayan children of the Yucatán had also asked children about the Sun, because there too, the Sun is a god. As is the case in many Mayan communities, the blending of Christianity and traditional religious practices and beliefs is quite common among the Luo. Which belief or practice is invoked often depends upon the circumstance.

As I listened to the professor describe God's eye, I was struck again by the strange intermingling of visibility and invisibility, of seeing or not. The ancestors are remembered in bodily—visible—form and "seen" in some sense in a person's dreams. Otherwise they are known in spirit form—invisible—after death, indirectly, by the help or troubles they instigate. On the other hand, the Sun itself is visible, but also a god. And the Sun's light makes seeing possible in the first place, if not for people, then for God. In both the ancestors and the Sun, the visible form blends with invisible personalities—that is, with a theory of mind, if not their essence or soul. As we found with the children in Louisville, relationships can take deep and abiding form with the invisible.

In addition to asking children about invisible friends, I would ask them about ancestors and the Sun.

Sadly, the first night in the village where we interviewed underlined how near the ancestors are to the hearts and homes of people. I awoke to music. A neighbor had died. Friends and relatives had gathered and they sang and drummed—interrupted only by wails—all through the night and into the next day, when they buried their loved one on their land. It was sad, beautiful, powerful, and so different from a US funeral home service. Death stays near, bodies stay home. I wondered what it would be like to have my relatives buried in my yard. Mine are spread out over several states in cemeteries. What would it mean to have the dead so near, reminding me of the lives of my ancestors?

In the morning, David and I met Oguda and Owaga Ochieng, twin brothers, in their twenties, who said to call them Ken and Ben. They had grown up in the village and could translate from the Luo language that the children would speak into English and vice versa. Children here eventually learn both English and Swahili in school, the two official languages of Kenya, but they speak only Luo at home and in the younger grades. As I explained the study to Ben and Ken, they stared at me with a look I feared meant, "Is this guy out of his mind?" Having told people in my own culture of academia about the research, I had seen the look plenty of times. "Did I hear you right, you ask children about invisible friends?" But my fear subsided when Ben told me his own invisible-friend story, how he had had such a friend as a child. In his case the line between imaginary friends and invisible ancestors blurred. That is, when Ben was a child of five or six, he had a good friend—the visible kind—that he played with. But the friend died. Not long after, Ben explained, the boy came back, invisibly, to be with him and they often played, talked, and hung out together. In one sense, the invisible friend was very much like Quack-Quack or Crystal, but in another sense, like the ancestors, he was rooted in an unimaginary source.

───────────

With Ben's and Ken's help, David and I interviewed over one hundred children between the ages of three and eight years. We first chatted with the children individually about friends in general: "Do you have any friends? What do you like to do with your friends?" Children smiled and readily described the games, reading, talking, and general playing they liked to do with their friends. And then came the big question: "Some children have friends that nobody else can see. They are invisible. Do you have any friends that nobody else can see?" Most did not, so we moved on to the theory-of-mind tasks.

But several said yes. When they did, we gently scrutinized, asking several questions: "You do? What's the name of your friend that nobody else can see? Tell me about [name of IF]. What do you like to do with this friend? Are you sure nobody else can see this this friend? Do you know what *invisible* means? Is your friend invisible?" The cognitive science side of me was afraid of two types of false-positive answers. On the one hand, as Marjorie Taylor suggests, children might say they have invisible friends just to be cooperative. On the other hand, the question could be misunderstood in various ways. For example, in one case a child named a friend whom nobody else could see because the friend had moved away. In another case, a girl named a boy that she secretly had a crush on. But Ken and Ben were great with the children and brilliant at the process of clarifying how the child interpreted the question.

In the end, twenty-three of the children (21 percent) maintained that they indeed had an invisible friend—not counting one seven-year-old boy who did not have one at the time of the interview but volunteered that he had had one when he was younger. Boys were as likely as girls to have one, and age was not a significant factor for predicting whether a child had an invisible friend.

Though the prevalence of invisible friends among these children is in the same statistical neighborhood as some previous studies elsewhere, I do not fixate too heavily on the percentages. As mentioned earlier, several factors can alter the results: who is asked, at what age, whether stuffed animals are included, and whether the child currently has the IF, to name a few contingencies. There are enough ambiguities and enough room for misunderstanding working within one's native culture that I don't think we can be overly confident about pinpointing the percentage of children who have them in another.

My questions were more fundamental: Do children in cultures very different from Louisville, Kentucky, even have anything like imaginary friends? Does the phenomenon of invisible friends exist in a place like western Kenya? After our interviews, I am convinced that some Luo children did have them. If anything, percentages could be higher. Our scrutinizing—even deftly handled by our translators—may have discouraged some children who had them to say they did not. Or had we asked all the children whether they had ever had an invisible friend, as some studies have, the percentages could have been much higher as well.

One aspect of the interviews, though, was very consistent with our Louisville study. When children described what they liked to do with the invisible friend, most pointed to the world of play. Other answers involved the ordinary activities of their lives or of the adult world: eating together, learning and writing, walking, fishing, cooking, and one three-year-old responded that he and his friend take care of the cattle together. I asked Ben whether it was possible that a three-year-old would be involved with actually taking care of cattle, and Ben said no way. Nearly all the invisible friends were human, but one child had an elephant as hers. Another child, a six-year-old girl, made a great point about her invisible friend, Emma, one I had not thought to ask about. She said nobody could see her friend except for God. God could see Emma.

Though we did not ask other children whether God could see their invisible friends, we did ask other questions about God's knowledge. As with the children in the initial study, we started with questions about invisible friends and followed with theory-of-mind tasks. But unlike the Louisville study, we conducted only two of them. Because everything we did had to be translated, we simplified. Compared to the other two tests we carried out in Louisville, the surprising-contents (rocks in the box) task is much simpler and faster. Both the background-knowledge (scribbles) and occluded-picture (elephant on ball) tasks required asking children about the knowledge of all the agents twice: once before the reveal and once after. In the crayon box test, we only had to ask children once, "What would your best friend think is in the box?" But we faced a challenge: would kids here know what a crayon box should contain in the first place? David didn't think they would. (We later confirmed he was right. We had brought crayons and invited any children with invisible friends to draw a picture, but they all declined—they were not well practiced at drawing in general, let alone with these waxy sticks.) David thought the bigger issue was the box itself. Even if they had used crayons before, the children were not exposed to much packaging of any sort. It was the same issue that led Knight to use a tortilla container with Mayan kids. So what was the equivalent to a crayon box or tortilla container in rural Kenya? Something familiar enough to create a surprise? David wasn't sure.

The night before we were to begin the interviews we still hadn't figured out what we would use, until David fired up his one-burner stove to cook dinner. Matches! All the kids would know matches and matchboxes because everyone cooked either over a fire or with a similar propane-fueled burner. And he had plenty of matchboxes right there at home that we could use. I liked the idea but was a little concerned that the box did not actually depict any matchsticks on the outside, only a rhinoceros. "They'll know." David assured. So we put tiny pebbles in matchboxes.

"What do you think is in this box?" The children said, "Matches." And they were indeed surprised when we showed them the true contents of pebbles. Like the Louisville children, we asked what a friend, a dog, and God would think is in the box, as well as their invisible friend, if they had one. In addition, we asked children about two others: the ancestors and the Sun.

As simple as this test is, the other test we used was even simpler. We showed the children a cloth bag and asked whether they knew the contents. The bag was plain and generic, no markings or other indication of what was inside. It bulged, so clearly something was in there, but the kids had no way of knowing what.

"Do you know what's inside this bag?" Some children said no immediately. Many guessed, but when asked what, they quickly admitted to not knowing. We then asked whether the other figures would know the contents. The test is called a *knowledge-ignorance task* because we never showed the children what was inside the bag. This too was a relatively quick and easy test to carry out even through translation. But that is not the primary reason I used it.

I included it because a study among Orthodox children in Greece found young children answering as Piaget would predict, egocentrically. It too utilized two different types of tests, one in which children were shown the contents of a box and another in which children never knew. When three- and four-year-olds were shown the contents, they thought others would know. But when the children did not know, they thought others, including God, would not know. If a three-year-old didn't know, they thought nobody knew, not even God! The authors interpret this finding as demonstrating that before children develop a robust theory of mind—that is, before they understand the limits of human knowing—they treat God just like a human (specifically, like themselves) as egocentrism predicts.

None of the three tests we used in Louisville created a condition of ignorance. All the children learned the secret: what the whole picture was, what the scribbles meant, that rocks were in the crayon box. Maybe that's why the young children were quick to attribute knowledge to others: they were just being egocentric. I wanted to see whether Luo children would respond as the Greek children did.

The results were far more complex than those in the Greek study. The answers for the false-belief test were similar to those in both the Greek and Louisville studies. Younger children tended to attribute knowledge to all the figures—ordinary humans and dogs, extraordinary spirits and gods—indiscriminately. For example, 75 percent of the three-year-olds thought their best friends would know rocks were actually in the match- box, while all the oldest children, the eight-year-olds, said that their best friends would think matches were in the box. Age mattered. However, age did not matter significantly for answers about God—children at all ages tended to say God would know rocks were in the box. "God created everything," a six-year-old girl reasoned, "so will know." In addition, much like our study and the Mayan one, the Sun, ancestors, and invisible friends were "in between." The children who understood their best friends would be fooled and think matches were in the box said the Sun, ancestors, and invisible friends were more likely to know rocks were actually in the box than the best friends, but less likely to know than God. A six-year-old boy who said the Sun will know what's in the matchbox offered, "The Sun has light that can go inside, so will know." Another child the same age said, "Ancestors see the same as God."

In short, we found cross-cultural consistency in responses for a false-belief test that includes invisible, extraordinary beings.

But the second task was the real test for egocentrism: would the young children attribute ignorance across the board when they did not know the contents of the bag? No, not at the level the Greek study found. For example, half the three-year-olds said their (visible) friend and a dog would know what's in the bag. They could have been guessing, but they were not answering egocentrically. More impressive, over three-quarters of these youngest said that God would know—this is right after admitting that they themselves did not know.

However, there were some slight differences between the results of the two types of tests. When children knew the contents of the box, they were more likely to say others would know. Except for God. Unlike the Greek study, the Luo children believed that God would know in either test.

As I've continued to reflect upon these results, it makes sense that knowing the surprise—rocks are in the matchbox—would bump up children's tendency to think others will know too. One theory is that once a young child knows something, it is difficult for them to suppress this knowledge and it overwhelms their budding ability to reason about other minds. In fact, we asked some of the young children afterwards what they thought was in the matchbox when they first saw it. Many of them said that they thought rocks were in the box even before they were shown. Their new knowledge overwrote their memory. Here, there is likely a connection to the development of executive function. *Executive function* is a catchall term for the set of cognitive skills that allows children to plan, focus attention, and oversee their own behavior. Just as young children often act impulsively—they see a ball rolling into the road and run after it without looking—they may also sometimes think impulsively. They see rocks in a box and think others will know rocks are in the box too. But in the bag test there is nothing to suppress, nothing to override their reasoning about other minds.

So it makes sense that children generally can pass a knowledge-ignorance test before they pass the false-belief test. Primatologists have even found chimpanzees capable of understanding ignorance, but they have not found evidence that nonhumans understand false belief. Appreciating that others have wrong information appears to be more complex than understanding that others simply don't have information.

Even so, I am not convinced the tendency to assume others know what we know ever goes completely away. I am aware of it in myself, especially in teaching. As an overschooled professor, I constantly catch myself using peculiar terms, or worse, jargon, not because I'm showing off fancy words I may know or because they're the most helpful. I do so because I'm on a linguistic roll lecturing and simply assume students know what the words mean. I think they know rocks are in the box.

David and I returned to Nairobi and met up with Amy. They were heading to Tanzania for a few days of vacation before returning to the US. David took me to a small party among some friends, a mix of ex-pats and locals he and Amy had gotten to know through their work. I was talking with a couple and they asked about the research we were doing. After I explained it and our findings, I asked for confirmation, "Do you think kids here have invisible friends?"

One of them, a woman originally from a northern part of Kenya, said, "Oh yes, I'm sure of it."

The man she was dating, from the US, seemed surprised at the quick response and said, "Really? Why are you so sure?"

"Because I had one," she said. She described how she had had an invisible friend from the time she was eight until her young teenage years. Complicating matters, she added, "He was a white boy."

―――――――――――――――

From Kenya, I had the chance to interview more children in Malawi. With the help of a former student and now friend, Fletcher Padoko, we interviewed over two hundred children in rural southern Malawi, near the city of Balaka. For several years Fletcher and his wife, Sarah (also a graduate from our school), had encouraged me to come visit them. The invisible friend project gave me a great reason to do so. Fletcher is a well-loved leader in the area, has utilized his own ancestral land to build schools and farms that feed the mind with learning and feed the body with grains, vegetables, and goats. He is trusted by the children and families of the surrounding villages, and to many he is an angel of mercy in the flesh. Like Kenya, Malawi is composed of multiple ethnic groups, but not nearly as many since Malawi and its population are so much smaller. Most villages are not ethnically monolithic, and the children we interviewed came from five different ethnic groups: Chewa, Yao, Lomwe, Nyanja, and Sena. In addition, this provided a chance to hear from children outside of a Christian background because many of them were Muslim. Still loaded with cross-cultural questions, I was eager to see whether religious differences would show up in relation to imaginary friends or in relation to how children thought about invisible or divine minds.

The short answer: they did not.

―――――――――――――――

We used the same procedures as we used in Kenya: asking whether children had a friend nobody else could see, followed by the two theory-of-mind tests. In fact, the same procedures were used in all four countries where I eventually interviewed. In Malawi, we started with some of the older children, who are easier to interview. They are less distracted and often take less time thinking about their answers. We were even able to interview children as old as twelve years of age, many of whom spoke some English. This let us double-check whether our questions were making sense and whether the protocol for the theory-of-mind tasks was clear. Beyond that, I was curious. What would older children say about having "friends nobody else can see"?

Two hundred and twenty children later, we were done.

We found fifty-seven children total, across all the ages, telling us about their invisible friends. That is a rate of 26 percent. The age of the child did not affect the rate significantly. That is, twelve-year-olds were as likely as three-year-olds to have an invisible friend, boys as likely as girls, and Muslims as likely as Christians. At 26 percent, the rate is higher than in the Kenya study (21 percent), but the difference is not statistically significant.

With so many children telling us about their imaginary friends, I was feeling even more confident about the answer to one of my primary questions: children in places very different from Louisville (or the US generally or Europe or Australia) indeed have them. The phenomenon is not restricted to the world's wealthier nations.

Even so, play itself was a big theme. The vast majority of the Malawi children who had invisible friends described playing with them. Several described playing football (soccer) or netball (similar to basketball and played mostly by girls and women in Malawi). As with soccer, if the kids didn't have an actual ball, they'd substitute with rags wound as tightly as possible. In addition to the ball sports, one budding track star liked to practice the long jump with his imaginary friend.

Some children described carrying out chores and other everyday activities with their invisible friends: drawing water from the community well, cooking, eating nsima (a doughy cornmeal dish served with most meals), carrying the imaginary friend around like a baby, talking, and generally visiting together, reminiscent of children playing house or with dolls in the US. While I did not see dolls or stuffed animals in Malawi, Fletcher described how children would sometimes make little figures for play out of mud. This time of year, well south of the equator, I did not witness this because it was the dry season—no mud.

In general, I was impressed by the way two sides of pretend play emerged in their descriptions. On the one hand, invisible friends were companions in general play, sports, and games; on the other, they were companions while doing chores or practicing adult roles in the society. Even in the absence of dolls, stuffed animals, or toys, children used whatever props available to construct a world of play. Those materials could be a rag soccer ball, netball post, mud, or the figures and representations of their imaginations.

Names were particularly fascinating in Malawi and revealing of the many historical influences upon the country. People's names cross several languages and cultures; some, such as Noah, Elizabeth, or Ruth, are rooted in the Bible and its Hebrew or Greek, while other names, such as Hawa or Shahida, are Arabic. Yet names did not necessarily follow religious lines; for example, a Christian boy might have the Arabic name Sayid. Reflecting both national languages, many names are English and more are from Chichewa; other names derive from one of the several other ethnolinguistic groups a child is from. Names such Precious or Gift are common, either in English or in the indigenous equivalent. And many children have names from a combination of languages, such as David Banda, the adopted son of the singer

Madonna. All these various influences showed up in the names children gave their invisible friends: Linda, Mercy, Eric, Mary, Ishmael, and Priscilla, but also Dalitso (Blessing in Chichewa), Yamikani (Praise), Thoko (Thanks), Pemphero (Prayer), Alinafe (God Is with Us), or Tiyanjane (Let Us Unite). The names of the imaginary friends reflected the same interplay of culture, religion, and family as the names of the children themselves. I was particularly charmed by the name of Yami's invisible friend. The five-year-old girl's friend was Secret. I was confused at first. "It's English, professor," the translator, a young man named MacDonald, explained, "when you don't tell something you know." And he explained that it was a common name in Malawi. But to my mind, an imaginary friend named Secret ranks up there with see-through Crystal.

One name of an invisible friend, John Chilembwe, surprised even Fletcher and Sarah. I asked why, and Fletcher asked if I had a 500-kwacha bill in my wallet. The kwacha is the currency of Malawi. I pulled one out, the equivalent of a little over a US dollar at the time. John Chilembwe's image was on one side. Sarah explained that he was a national hero, a Baptist minister who in the early twentieth century organized resistance to the British colonial system and is currently celebrated on John Chilembwe Day every January 15 in Malawi. But to one eleven-year-old girl, he was an invisible companion.

Another name of an invisible friend baffled even MacDonald, who had otherwise been able to explain to me the significance of any name. He and I were talking with a six-year-old, a boy who liked to go to the well with his imaginary friend to draw water. "And what is the name of your friend nobody else can see?" The boy answered, and MacDonald responded with a version of "Huh?" I heard the name clearly but waited. The boy repeated the name, one completely foreign to MacDonald, and once again he said, "Huh?" Then he asked again in Chichewa, "What is the name?" The six-year-old said it one more time, and MacDonald repeated the name. The child nodded affirmation. MacDonald then said to me, "Professor, I have never heard this name before and don't know what language it is. He says the invisible friend's name is Harvey." I smiled.

Later, as I tried to explain the significance of the name to the research team, I learned another valuable cross-cultural lesson. Describing a grown man having an invisible friend who is a six-foot, three-and-a-half-inch rabbit and shapeshifting Celtic fairy is difficult. "Huh?"

"Do you know what's inside this bag?" As in Kenya, we asked children about the knowledge of another child, God, an imaginary friend if they had one, and an animal, in this case a chicken. We switched animals from dog to chicken because—like a girl had in the US— some of the older children in Kenya had said that a dog would be able to smell the contents. We thought maybe children would think of a chicken (a food source) as less able to do so. In consultation with my hosts, we switched from asking about ancestors to a slightly more generic *spirits* as potential in-between figures. Ancestors are important in Malawi as well, and ancestors are spirits. But *spirits* could refer to anyone's ancestors, not just one's own, as that aspect or essence of a person that survives after death. Because of their circumstances, these children may or may not have heard a lot of talk about their own ancestors, but talk about spirits more generally was very common. In addition, we asked about angels. Angels and demons are both very much part of the general belief system across religions. Had we been talking with adults, I might have included demons. But since we were talking with children, I chose to stick to angels only, fearing that a strange-talking foreign man even mentioning demons could disturb some children.

True to our hunch, children treated angels, spirits, and invisible friends as in between. Many of the children who passed the test—who said a chicken or human would not know the contents of the bag or matchbox—said that their invisible friend would know. But God was even more likely to know. Angels and spirits were in the same in-between territory as imaginary friends. As was true in Kenya, the Malawi children also received religious education both in school and in church or mosque, and sometimes the children added explanations for the divine mind accordingly: "because God knows everything" or "because God made everything." The larger lesson, again, seems to be that such teachings about God are learned easily by children, unlike learning binary code. However, there is no reason to believe that children are being taught anything about imaginary friends or the mental capacities of such pretend companions, directly or indirectly. Parents are not teaching their children that imaginary friends "know what's in your heart" or "made everything" or "know everything." And still, between a quarter and a third of children who understood the limits of human minds attributed special abilities to their imaginary friends.

Between Kenya and Malawi, I found myself increasingly persuaded that children indeed get a running start at believing God or angels and spirits know in special ways. When children are very young, the assumption is that any other mind knows. For example, the three-year-olds in Malawi said that another child would know rocks were in the box at the high rate of 71 percent. And over half (58 percent) even said that a chicken would know. (And several of the older kids still thought the chicken could smell through the containers.) Rates for the other figures were even higher, all hovering around 80 percent.

As I crunched these numbers, I tried a thought experiment: What did I assume about other minds when I was three or four? I scanned my early childhood memories and couldn't tell much from them. I realized how silly the exercise was, unscientific, untrustworthy, and unreplicable. I gave up.

Then Miss Lois popped into my mind. "Romper bomper, stomper boo, tell me, tell me, tell me, do. Magic Mirror, tell me today, have all my friends had fun at play?" Miss Lois was the host of the syndicated television show *Romper Room* in St. Louis, where I grew up. At the end of the show, she would hold up the Magic Mirror, say these words, and see all the boys and girls watching from home. "I see Joe had a special day today, and Sue and David and Rebecca had a special day, and I see Barbara and Chris. . . . " One morning—as I remember it—instead of getting ready for nursery school, I was lying sick on our couch watching Miss Lois and the Magic Mirror. I heard, " . . . and I see Bradley is home sick today." Four years old at the time, I believed in the powers of the Magic Mirror. Still in my thought-experiment mode, I then realized how easily I bought into the notion that Santa could know what I wanted for Christmas (even if I told only my folks), or when I was a little older, that the Tooth Fairy could know when I had lost a tooth or, for that matter, know when I was asleep enough to leave a dime under my pillow without being seen. I assumed these other minds knew.

Then again, as I thought about it, in these examples I knew. They are equivalent to knowing rocks are in the box. I knew I was home sick, what I wanted for Christmas, or that I'd lost a tooth. It could simply be egocentrism, as Piaget described. *I know, others will know.*

So back to the numbers. The better test for egocentrism is the knowledge-ignorance test, the bulging bag, because children never learn what is inside. In this test we found the young Malawi children attributing knowledge to other children at the same rate as the false belief test, at 71 percent, unegocentrically. *I don't know, but others do.*

I went to East Africa with a headful of cultural questions but could focus only on two: first, would these children have invisible friends, and second, how do the children think about the invisible minds of others? The answer to the first is yes, some do have invisible friends. The answer to the second question is that even young children, Christian and Muslim alike, easily thought of God as knowing in extraordinary ways, a result in conflict with the Greek study. Along the way I found children's reasoning about the gods large and small—including the Sun, the ancestors, and invisible friends—was more complicated, varying according to the kind of test used. But the cross-cultural evidence was growing. The egocentrism-to-logical-thinking picture of child development was not holding up. At the same time, I wondered why children would assume others have knowledge. Is it something about our deeply social minds? Our mind-reading minds? I didn't have a good answer.

"Made paper airplanes," I jotted in my notebook, "from leftover interview protocols." I was sitting on the porch of Fletcher's house, looking over my notes and through my folder of interviews. I was done, but my mind still felt in work mode. A couple of kids showed up, playing under a nearby tree, laughing, running around, having fun. I noticed in the folder several blank copies of the interview protocol. I had brought more than needed. I unstapled one and proceeded to make a paper airplane with one of the pages. Even before I finished, the kids came over and stared at the strange folds I was making in the paper. I threw the plane; it flew a good fifteen feet. The children laughed and ran to retrieve it. I thought they would try to throw it back, but they brought it to me to throw again. I did, and we repeated the game.

The next time the child handed the plane to me, I didn't take it. I pantomimed what he should do, pretending to throw. He tried but let go too late and it hit the ground immediately. I picked it up, handed it to him, pointing the tip up high. Success. The other child ran after and they began throwing it back and forth. "Joy," I recorded later, "two kids—then twenty." While the two played with the plane, other children started gathering and I hustled to make more, turning interview questions into wings. Soon paper planes and joy flew everywhere. Their play got me playing, and I could think of no better cause for leftover copies of very serious, empirical tools for cognitive investigation.

CHAPTER 8

GODS AND GODSIBBS

*"There ought to be a book written about me,
that there ought!"*

NOTEBOOK: "I know she has an IF." As I reflected upon the night before, in the Everest Hotel of Kathmandu, I wrote these words. I was now waiting in the domestic airport for my flight to western Nepal, to the city of Pokhara. "Had a wonderful meal at the restaurant at the hotel, with live music and a couple of 'Everest' beers." At a table between the band and me was a family that appeared to be at least three generations, the youngest being a little girl who was likely three or four years old. She was dancing to the music. At one point she half-danced and half-skipped over to a fountain inside the restaurant and I noticed her lips moving. I thought she was singing, but when the song ended, she stopped dancing but continued moving her lips. She stood at the edge of the fountain, eyed the water, then turned and, as I wrote it, started "talking away to nobody." Then she stopped, appeared to listen, nodded, stuck her hand into the water, and smiled as if looking for approval from her invisible pal.

I was going to Pokhara, Nepal, because a friend from the US, Karen, connected me to an organization that could help facilitate the research. When asked about my choices of countries for this project, my reply is simple: "Opportunism." In research literature, it would be called "sampling by convenience." True enough for my research, but I stumble over this phrase that sounds like bopping down to the local corner store for some bread. In the original grant proposal, I suggested the guiding principle would be to interview children in places "as different from Louisville, Kentucky, as feasible." With Nepal, I succeeded. Not only is Nepal geographically far away, half a spin of the globe from Kentucky, religiously it is very different. Until 2006, Nepal was officially a Hindu kingdom and the overwhelming majority of people still are Hindu. Buddhists represent the only sizeable religious minority, with a handful of Christians, Muslims, and Sikhs scattered through the population. In addition to asking children about invisible friends, I was also eager to explore how Nepali children's theory of the minds of the gods and goddesses would compare to Christian and Muslim children's theory of mind for their god. Would Shiva or Parvati or Laxmi know what's in the box?

Pokhara is a relatively large city with a tourist district along a beautiful lake flanked by hills and ultimately the majestic Himalayas (though mostly hidden while I was there because of the monsoons). Pokhara's streets are loaded with shops and restaurants with signs in both Nepali and English, if not Chinese, Japanese, and Italian as well. I was struck by how many businesses were named for religious figures: Laxmi Ice Cream, Ganesh Kayaks, and Buddha Airlines, for example. The juxtaposition of divinity with such prosaic commercial enterprises was jarring at first to my church-and-state-and-business-divided brain. I tried to imagine Louisville with a Jesus Christ Ice Cream Parlor or Lord of Hosts Canoe Rentals. In between the shops, on corners, at the base of trees, in walls, were sharper expressions of devotion. Statues of Hindu deities and versions of the

Buddha appeared whichever way I turned. Some were old and worn down, others were newer with elaborate details. Most had splashes of color—bright yellows and reds—smeared on them as part of a *puja* (worship) ritual.

Looking around, I was thrown back to my own childhood. As a Presbyterian growing up in a Catholic neighborhood in the 1960s, I was baffled yet fascinated by the statuary and monuments, the saints and angels, the candles and incense, by all the tangible representations of invisible powers I lived among. These were foreign to my tradition, an iconoclastic Protestant world that broke from Catholicism, shunning representations of divinity and continuously fearing idolatry if not Catholics themselves. With the emphasis upon Scripture, my tradition was one teeming with words rather than angels or saints. Even the rite of communion—bread and wine serving as a visible sign of Christ's invisible grace—was reserved until adolescence and the onset of abstract thought. What would it be like, I wondered, if I'd not thought of all the monuments and statues as icons or idols? What if in my heart and mind these had been more porous to the sacred?

I saw some children kicking a can around in a makeshift soccer game. I thought that surely kids here have lots of invisible friends. Not only are homes and neighborhoods teeming with gods, but the streets, shops, trees, and incense-filled air are as well.

Interviewing children about invisible friends presented no special challenges in a polytheistic culture that I could see. I was reasonably confident that asking about *invisible* (rather than *imaginary*) friends helped get around the possible confusion Antonia Mills discovered in India, where the companions were considered friends from a previous life. In addition, the Nepali adults with whom I discussed the project seemed to know what I was talking about. To top the matter off, I later discovered through my interview translator, Ram, that *Foster's Home for Imaginary Friends* had made its way to Pokhara, at least to his household. A thoughtful young man in his twenties, Ram is a photographer and loves the Nashville rock band Kings of Leon. He is no stranger to Western culture. I asked him if he had had an imaginary friend. "No," he answered quickly, followed by a laugh. Did he know anybody who did? He thought for a moment, then shook his head no.

The greater interview challenge had to do with the question "What would God think?" There are so many deities to choose from. In Hinduism, some get more attention than others, depending upon geography, schools of thought, traditions, households, and more. Some have more power than others or, more accurately, have different realms of power. Ganesh clears obstacles. Laxmi is a goddess of wealth and prosperity. Shiva is a destroyer but also represents goodness and purity. Nothing is simple. Vishnu is a ruler and protector who has had several human incarnations, including Krishna. Like Jesus in Christianity, this makes Krishna a god as well. Some would say all the gods and goddesses are aspects of Brahman, the Absolute Oneness, more a philosophical or metaphysical concept than a typical, personified deity. To children, Brahman could easily be confused with the similar-sounding Brahma, the Creator. So the question was which deity we should ask about.

In the end, I decided to let the children choose. When posing the theory-of-mind questions, we used the generic term for "a deity" or "a god." The only difference from the other countries was that afterwards I asked, "Which deity were you thinking of?" I was curious. Would answers coalesce around two or three of the gods or goddesses, or would the children name lots of different ones? Would the deity named make a difference for the theory-of-mind tasks? Perhaps some gods would know what's in the matchbox while others would not. Monotheists load God up with all the divine powers imaginable. But polytheism tends to spread the wealth around, so to speak, attributing some powers to this god, others to that goddess. So I wondered whether the power to know in special ways might get pinned to one or some deities but not others.

I also wondered whether there were anything like angels or other in-betweens I could quiz children about. Karen's husband, Surya, from Nepal, suggested the *pari* (sometimes spelled *peri*), winged, fairylike creatures who are said to populate the earth and skies, something like nymphs. He explained they were not tied particularly to Hinduism or Buddhism, which made them good candidates. I later discovered that stories of the pari likely migrated from what is now Iran, before Islam, and even before Zoroastrianism, and the English words *fairy* and *paradise* are linguistic descendants. Moreover, many of the stories and images associated with the pari involve crystal: sometimes they are depicted as wearing crystal glasses; other stories involve their glass palaces on mountaintops; and in some stories they are said to be as translucent as water. Crystal! It makes me wonder whether Cora's translucent friend had a glass palace towering atop the invisible Himalayas of her imagination.

<hr />

"He says that he and his brother have them," Ram reported. We were in a small village outside the city talking with a boy seven years old. He explained that they have a whole other family they play with together. "A mother and father, an older brother and a younger sister." The boy smiled.

"Are you sure he's not just talking about his actual family?" I questioned. Ram asked whether the family was visible.

"He says no, he and his brother just made them up and like to play with them."

The boy was one of the first children we interviewed, and I was as moved by the sweetness of these brothers playing "family" as I was excited with the promise of more stories to come. With so many deities and fairies, with the statuary and temples, and with fuzzy lines between secular and sacred realms, I knew we would hear about loads of see-through friends.

I was wrong. This little boy was one of only five children who said they had invisible friends. That is 5 of 101, mostly Hindu (9 were Buddhist, 3 Christian), for a rate of just under 5 percent. The five who did have them were convincing, so I believe the phenomenon occurs among Nepali children, but the question is, Why such a low rate? One of the factors that may have generated a low rate was age. These children ranged from five to eight years old. We tried to interview three- and four-year-olds, but they were simply too shy—or, more accurately, untalkative.

In their 1990 book about childhood imagination, *The House of Make-Believe*, Dorothy and Jerome Singer identify the preschool years as the "high season of make-believe." While we found plenty of older children with invisible friends, it still makes sense that children after three or four years might be more reticent about admitting they have imaginary friends precisely because of their theory of mind. If children at five or six years are realizing more fully that others have a perspective different from their own, if they are becoming more aware of what others think, we could expect an increase in self-consciousness. In short, the developing theory of mind could make a child less and less willing to reveal having imaginary friends—that is, if the context doesn't support them.

Before I had even begun to interview, I was out to dinner with some folk I'd met through the research and we were joined unexpectedly by a couple of young women who had been working with children and families in the area for a nongovernmental agency addressing issues of poverty and education. They were intrigued by the project but not optimistic about our finding a lot of imaginary friends. Their pessimism came from asking children to draw. Most didn't know what to do with the crayons, but if they did start using them, they were as likely as not to just draw straight lines or create a grid. "Kids just don't draw."

"Even so," I wondered out loud with them, "comfort with crayons or drawing isn't exactly the same as imagination."

They agreed, but then another dinner partner, a Nepali man who had spent time in the US, jumped into the discussion. He said, gently, "I'm not sure either, but here's another example. Let's say I'm a child at home and I'm reading a story from a book or magazine. My parents will probably say something like, 'It's good that you are reading, but why aren't you reading your textbooks from school?' I think this would be typical of many homes here."

I still don't know whether the imagination as such is discouraged or not. But if there were a general emphasis on this kind of realism, in schools or homes, that discourages children from sharing stories or characters born of their own fantasy, it could help explain the low percentages we found. Marjorie Taylor and Stephanie Carlson found parental attitudes among US Christians played an important role in the imaginative lives of children. In general they found that mainstream Christian parents tended to support fantasy play of all kinds in young children, including the incorporation of Santa Claus and the Easter Bunny at Christmas and Easter, as well as support play with imaginary friends. But they found a different pattern among fundamentalist Christian parents. They often discouraged fantasy, including invisible friends, because they tended to associate fantasy with the occult; they worried that so-called imaginary friends could be demonic. The exception to this general rule among fundamentalist parents was Jesus, whom some of the children they interviewed named as their invisible friend.

The combination of age (developing theory of mind) and a context that discourages fantasy play could certainly make a difference. I've wondered as well about the role of visibility or invisibility. The divinities of

Nepal are so clearly visible everywhere. Perhaps the imagination aligns more fully with the rich sensory world of colors and smells, textures and sounds, much as most children in the US are drawn to playful props— dolls and models and stuffed animals—to animate their imaginations towards the visible world. I don't know. In the end I believe the case of imaginary friends among Nepali children remains open.

Who knows what? In addition to the extraordinary pari and deity, we asked children about their best friends and a mosquito. We asked about the insect for the same reason we asked about chickens in Malawi: I wanted to see how far this tendency to attribute knowledge to creatures would go and figured kids might place bugs farther down the knowledge ladder. Mosquitos are everywhere in Nepal, and with them, unfortunately, malaria, so children are well aware of the pest. We were trying to use an agent that potentially could be even more ignorant than a dog or chicken.

The results for the ordinary figures were quite consistent with the previous studies. Keep in mind, these children were older, five to eight years old. Nearly all (twenty-two of twenty-three) of the youngest children, the five-year olds, passed the knowledge-ignorance test, saying that their best friend would not know the contents of the bag. Of those twenty-two, all but three children said the mosquito would not know. I asked those three afterwards how the mosquito would know. One said, "A mosquito is so small, it could squeeze through the top of the bag" where it was tied with a drawstring. The other two children didn't offer a reason. While the five-year-olds overwhelmingly passed the bag test, only about half of them (47 percent) passed the false-belief test, responding that their best friend would think matches were in the box. The children were six, on average, before passing consistently, suggesting again that the ability to understand that someone else has wrong information is more complex than understanding that someone has no access to the information.

When it came to answers for a deity, children of all ages attributed knowledge at significantly high rates in both tasks. Over and over, the children who passed the tests (83 percent) answered that a deity would know the true contents of the bag or matchbox, while 67 percent said that the pari would know. Much like the ancestors and Sun in Kenya, spirits and angels in Malawi, the alux and Sun in the Yucatán, much like the invisible friends everywhere we interviewed, these translucent fairies were another in-between. They were more likely to know things an ordinary human or insect would not know but less likely than a deity. (Likewise, the few invisible friends we found in Nepal came out in between, but with so few, the percentages are meaningless.)

I had an answer to one question: Nepali children treated the generic concept of "a deity" similarly to the ways Christian and Muslim children in our previous studies thought about God. Still, it could have been that they all were thinking of the same god—say, Vishnu, one of the more prominent and powerful ones.

But they were not. When asked, "Which deity were you thinking of?" at the end of the interview, the eighty-nine Hindu children named thirteen different deities: Devi, Shiva, Ganesh, Laxmi, Ram, Saraswati, Krishna, Radha, Hanuman, Parvati, Vishnu, Durga, and Buddha. Yes, Buddha was named by two of the Hindu children, even as two of the nine Buddhist children named Hindu deities. Of the three Christian children, one named God, another Jesus, and the third said she was thinking of Ganesh. I checked whether the naming of any particular deity predicted yes answers more than others—for example, whether Shiva was more likely to know than Parvati. But the particular god or goddess named did not matter—they were all very likely to know the contents of the bag or matchbox, according to these children.

The picture painted by the results among these children is one in which special powers of knowing are not the sole property of a certain god or particular goddess, but the stuff of any divine mind.

—————————————

The day before leaving Pokhara I gained a rare glimpse. The sky cleared and the Himalayas towered above the city, white tops sparkling in the sky. Amazing. I imagined Crystal playing with her pari friends in a see-through castle atop the ridge before me. I waved.

A year later, I'd be writing Cora about her friend from the shores of the Caribbean.

—————————————

Cora,

We interviewed today—several children had IFs. One was of a girl, 7, who was named "Crystal"! She made a drawing too, so will send that to you when I have a scanner.

Hope you're doing well.

Love, Dad

This email to my adult daughter was sent from the small town of Guayacanes, where I was staying, just outside the capital city of Santo

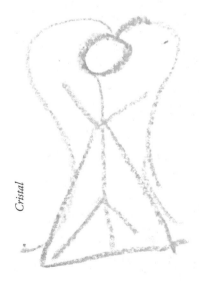

Cristal

Domingo in the Dominican Republic. I eventually found a scanner.

According to Maria, the seven-year-old who drew this picture, Cristal had been in her life for "mucho tiempo" (a long time). They liked to play together and lately had been playing card games, though I didn't think to ask who usually wins.

Maria was the last child we interviewed in the capital. I had enlisted the help of Jo Ella Holman, a friend from the US who currently lives in the Dominican Republic. To that point we had interviewed nearly seventy children during the previous weeks, about half in Santo Domingo and the other half in a rural area a couple hours north. Before completing the research, we would interview another twenty in the city of La Romana, along the southern coast an hour outside the capital. All had gone well. First, I know enough Spanish that I could understand much more of what the children were saying than in any of the interviews since Louisville. We used translators all the same (in part because my broken Spanish would have been a distraction to the children). This allowed us to scrutinize the answers children gave with more confidence and clarity than in Kenya, Malawi, or Nepal. Second, children were happy to draw pictures. The only difficulty for some children, like eight-year-old Daniela, was deciding which of multiple IFs to draw. She landed on her two favorite, Jose and Sara. While the Dominican Republic is a poor nation compared to the US, the standard of living is much higher than in the other non-US places I'd been for the research. Crayons may not be in most homes, but they are not strange to schools, so the children had experience with them. Third, many of the adults and children were familiar with the idea of *amigos imaginarios*. Not only had *Foster's Home for Imaginary Friends* made it to the island, but the adults with whom I spoke about the project were not shy about sharing stories of imaginary friends—either those from their kids or from their own childhoods. Fourth, Dominicans by and large are not shy, period. Something in the water perhaps, or the bright sunshine? But even three- and four-year-olds were eager to talk with us.

The day after sending her the email, I spoke with Cora via Skype. We laughed about the ways both she and Cristal had found their way into Spanish-speaking cultures, Cora through a college semester in Chile. Then, all of a sudden, Cora stopped laughing.

"What's wrong?" I asked.

"Nothing," she said. "I was just remembering our high school trip to the DR." She, along with her brother David and the youth group

Jose and Sara

of our church, had made a trip to the island a decade earlier. "Well, it's so beautiful there, and warm, maybe Crystal went too and just decided to stay!"

Between the three locations, we interviewed eighty-eight children, mostly three to seven years of age but a few eight-year-olds as well. We followed the same routine as before, asking children about friends, a best friend, and eventually whether they had a friend that nobody else could see. But because of the general cultural familiarity with the idea of imaginary friends, we followed their responses by asking whether they knew about IFs. While some of the youngest did not, virtually all the older children knew about them. "Yes, friends that are pretend. They are not real." The clarity was refreshing. If a child named a friend nobody else could see, we could ask whether it was imaginary. "Is Cristal an imaginary friend?" Yes she was, according to Maria.

Maria was not alone. Of the eighty-eight children, twenty-nine of them said they had an imaginary friend at the time of our conversation—over a third of them, 34 percent. This is a significantly higher rate than Kenya (21 percent) and Malawi (23 percent) for the same age group. And at 5 percent, it is no surprise that all three countries' rates are significantly higher than Nepal's. Since the children of Nepal were all five to eight years of age, I also compared only children of the same age from each country. The results were even more striking. Dropping the three- and four-year-olds from the samples slightly lowered the rates of Kenya (19 percent) and Malawi (22 percent), but in the Dominican Republic the rate went up to 44 percent. The older Dominican children were more likely to have imaginary friends.

These numbers gave me a lot to think about, and I continue to do so. Because I've found evidence for imaginary friends in all the places I went, I'm inclined to believe the potential for them transcends any particular culture. Something deep in the souls of young people is ready to befriend an invisible community of ducks and teapots and see-through humans. Imaginary friends don't appear to be limited to places that emphasize play and recreation or have the toys and props to help. At the same time, culture matters, whether the culture of a country, community, or household. Cultures may well support or discourage children's see-through companions and imaginative play. Invisible George has a place at the table or not. Quack-Quack is a mark of a rich imagination or a demonic temptation. Reading fiction is okay, but studying textbooks is what matters. And some cultures may simply tolerate such imaginative play, neither supporting nor discouraging it. This is my hunch about both Kenya and Malawi, where the rates of invisible friends did not differ significantly. They're the closest geographically, less than a thousand miles apart. And while very different in some ways, they are still the most culturally similar to each other of all the countries. In both places I found few props for play, but in neither did I find anything to discourage imaginative play or invisible friends. The Dominican Republic is less than a thousand miles from the US as well, and the cultural influence from the States is strong. For example, much of the television news and entertainment in the DR comes from Florida stations. It may only be a coincidence, but whatever makes children comfortable with crayon drawing may be related to the support of imaginary friends—nearly half the kids with them provided drawings.

With the relative clarity of communication in the DR, I decided to ask children who did not currently *have* an imaginary friend whether they *had* one when they were younger. I don't think the question was very useful with the young three- and four-year-olds. Except for one precocious child, the answers were always the same. If they said they did not have a friend nobody else could see, they also said no to the question "Did you *ever* have a friend nobody else could see, when you were younger?" This is not too surprising since young children's sense of narrative time—of "younger"—is still developing, not to mention their conscious memory-making. But the answers of the older children were different. Many of those who said that they did not currently have an invisible friend said that they used to have one or more and could name them. In all, thirty-one of the five- to eight-year-olds claimed either to have or to have previously had an imaginary friend, for a remarkable 57 percent.

This figure of 57 percent does not count the two children in this age range who named Jesus Christ as a friend nobody else can see or the two who named God. The Dominican Republic is overwhelmingly Christian and virtually all of the children we interviewed were as well. A seven-year-old boy, Marco, even identified God as his *best* friend. That was unique in all the interviews anywhere. When he said it, I thought of the biblical notion of becoming "a friend of God." Abraham is the supreme

example, but he is not alone. In the Wisdom of Solomon, wisdom is personified as a woman, a reflection of the eternal light of God. She comes to every generation and passes into holy souls and "makes them friends of God and prophets." On the outside, Marco appeared to be a thoughtful young boy, but I wondered how much more was going on in that holy soul. We eventually got the name of a visible friend to ask about, but when we asked Marco about invisible friends, he named Jesus. Because Jesús is a common boy's name in the Dominican Republic, we probed. Jesús could be a fellow seven-year-old or the deity, or he could be an imaginary duck. Marco said he knew what amigos imaginarios were, that they were "en tu cabeza" (in your head), but he didn't have one. He clarified further—his invisible friend was Jesús Cristo.

Many characteristics of invisible friends discovered elsewhere reappeared in the Dominican Republic. Several children had multiple see-through friends. I was particularly charmed by the drawing of six-year-old Corazón depicting her five imaginary companions whom she said had been around since she was one year old. They all like to paint and color together, watch movies, and in general "jugamos mucho" (we play a lot). Over and over, children employed some form of the verb *jugar* (play) when describing their imaginary friends: "We play dolls." "We play games." "We play all kinds of things." "We have fun." "We color."

"We play ball." "We play ball and we dance." Imaginary friends were most often humanish, but some children described animals. For example, three-year-old Sarah played with an invisible elephant. Unlike Kenya and Malawi, there are no elephants in the Dominican Republic, except perhaps in a zoo. Food came up as it did elsewhere: "We play and eat together." "We play in the park and eat ice cream." Some children were happy to share their imaginary friends while playing with others. Isabella, an eight-year-old girl, described how she shared Piescitos—whom she loved—with her friends. But, she admitted, her friends couldn't see him. She was learning English in school and to make it very clear to me, she used the English *love*. She then drew a picture of Piescitos and a separate one with his name in a heart.

The name Piescitos is curious, meaning something like "little feet." I consulted a friend of mine, Ada Asenjo, who grew up in the Dominican Republic and was also part of the interview team in the US study. She said Piescitos is not an actual name anyone would have officially, but it could be a nickname. She remembered a guy in her neighborhood growing up whom they called Brazos Largos (Long Arms). She added, "I never knew his actual name!"

We did not hear of any shapeshifters per se, but five-year-old Luis had two versions of Alejandro: "a little one and a big one." That interview took place in the town of La Romana, and when I heard of these friends of Luis, I went back through my notes and drawings because I thought I'd heard this before. I was right, sort of. A girl in the capital, Elizabeth, had Alejandra, the feminine version of the name. In fact, Elizabeth had two imaginary friends named Alejandra. One was a seven-year-old girl, like Elizabeth; the other Alejandra was six. Perhaps there is a cartoon

Two Alejandras

character somewhere, Alejandro or Alejandra, but I found no clues to this coincidence of names.

Some children who did not have imaginary friends told us about ones that their brothers or sisters had. Other children, like the little boy in Nepal, had whole pretend families. Seven-year-old Daria described an imaginary mother-daughter duo: Iris and her mother. Daria told us how Iris comes to school with her. But, she explained, Iris is "bad in school." She is "always looking out the window." When she said this, I wondered whether there had been some confusion. Was she really describing an imaginary friend and mother or visible ones or some odd combination? To clarify, we probed some more: "Can other people see Iris? Iris's mother?" Daria assured us that only she, Daria, could see them, and that Iris and her mother were only "en mi cabeza."

Despite similarities with invisible friends from other parts of the globe, a couple of them seemed to represent firsts in my research, both having to do with security. A five-year-old boy, Javier, described "una caja secreta" (a secret box) he had. We were never entirely clear whether this was simply a box that he kept hidden or some kind of miniature safe or even a toy cash register, since a cash register in a store can be called *una caja*. Regardless, money (pretend or otherwise) was involved, and this little boy's imaginary friend was a security guard who kept watch over the box and over him when he opened it. It was curious, but I didn't think too much about it until a few days later. I went into a bank to get some cash and I was stopped at the door by a very well-armed man to whom I tried to explain, in my poor Spanish, the reason for entering. I eventually succeeded, but after that, an imaginary guard for a child who is either hiding some treasure in a safe or playing store with a cash register made great sense. Besides, what better protection—a guard nobody else can see!

Another security-related description comes not from a child but from an adult. I was meeting with a small group of community leaders, some of whom were helping me organize interviews. We were in the home of Natalia, a young woman, barely five feet tall, who was pastor of a local congregation. I was explaining the project to them through a translator. They knew already that it had to do with child development, but they were curious about the connections to invisible beings. Natalia was in another part of the room getting cups together to serve us coffee. When I got to the part about amigos imaginarios, I heard Natalia gasp. I looked at her, worried I had just stepped into problematic territory. Maybe she, like some fundamentalist parents in the US, associates such invisible beings with the demonic. She asked whether we indeed were talking about imaginary friends, and I confirmed that we were. She then burst out laughing. "I had one," she explained, "named Nágive." She'd had Nágive from the time she was eight until she was twelve. Natalia described how, in those years, she walked from school to her grandmother's house. Nágive was a police officer and accompanied her, keeping her safe. Natalia was a bit embarrassed telling us the story, then surprised and tickled that a professor (from a church-based school in the US) would be studying something as odd as imaginary friends. "¿Soy loca?" She asked, only half kidding. She wanted to know—as many do—whether I thought this meant there was something wrong with her. I told her no and about all the kids all over the world I had talked with and about my own daughter and Crystal. Natalia stood a little taller.

Long after these interviews, I remembered one other instance of the theme of security among children's imaginary friends: a four-year-old boy named Loren in Louisville. I went back to the interview conducted by Lacey. Loren played with Tigris, a kung fu master from the *Kung Fu Panda* films. Tigris not only kept Loren safe but was teaching him the martial art. But Tigris wasn't Loren's only imaginary friend or protector. There was Thomas, an invisible alligator, who appeared when Loren was only two years old. His mother, recalling the origins of Thomas, said,

"I think at one point Loren was afraid of alligators. Then all of a sudden, instead of being afraid of them, he created Thomas, an alligator, and they became—" she interrupted herself, "—and Thomas became his friend." I replayed that sentence with its interruption a few times, pondering the rephrasing. She'd started to say "they became friends" but switched to "Thomas became his friend." Subtle, but it's as if using the word *they* might suggest that the reality status of the alligator and her son were the same. But she quickly moved on to describe another alligator, a female, Percy. Loren sometimes, Mom explained, refers to Thomas and Percy as his brother and sister. "And then there's Marshall. I'm not even sure if Marshall is an alligator, but he hangs out with us." Loren himself described playing together with these friends, having parties, how they help him with his schoolwork, and the way they practice both dance and kung fu moves, which he demonstrated for Lacey.

The interview reminded me of one of those dreams in which the person who represents a threat—maybe chasing you down the street or stopping you at a border—turns out to be friendly and helpful. A scary alligator becomes a protector, friend, sibling, helper, and dance partner. The psychologist Erik Erikson described the initial dilemma that every child faces in the world as trust versus mistrust. It is not enough to simply trust. Plenty of situations, people, and aspects of the world are worthy of some fear and trepidation, including actual alligators! Our species would not have survived on trust alone. The developmental, if not existential, challenge is to incorporate mistrust within a larger openness to life. This little boy, two at the time, navigated a way that did not allow fear to swallow up his ability to dance. A kung fu master may have helped, and I suspect his parents did too.

***

"What would Santa Claus think is in the box?" We followed our questions about invisible friends with the same two cognitive tasks we had used in Kenya, Malawi, and Nepal: the bag and matchbox tests (we likely could have used a crayon box here). Not only did we ask whether invisible friends—along with God, best friend, and dog—would know what's in the bag or box, we asked about angels and Santa Claus. As in Malawi, angels are part of the religious landscape of the island; as in the US, Dominican kids know and anticipate visits from Santa. The song says, "He knows if you've been bad or good." So would that mean he knows what's in the box? Then again, he lives so far away in the North Pole, and it was summertime; maybe he wouldn't be watching at the moment. Or maybe he was. As one child said of Jesus, "Even though he is way up in heaven, he can still see us from there." Would that be true of Santa?

Santa turned out to be unique among the in-betweens. Children said he would know at high rates, but only to a point. A comparison with angels is revealing. Nearly two-thirds of six-year-olds attributed knowledge to Santa and to angels. But by seven the rate is even higher for angels (86 percent) and it drops for Santa (40 percent). I was puzzled at first by this trend until one talkative seven-year-old offered, "Santa's not real." I realized that the results for Santa include some children who wanted to make sure we knew that they knew Santa is made up. But it probably included some children who still believed in him as well as others who were in on the ruse but played along anyway. Angels, on the other hand, are considered real, and the older a child was, the more likely the angelic mind was like God's mind.

In most other ways, the Dominican children's responses were similar to children's responses from the other countries. Younger children tended to attribute knowledge to all the figures at very high rates, while older children said that their best friend or dog would not know what was in the bag or box. Age mattered for those figures. But answers for God did not change with age. Overwhelmingly, children of any age answered that God or an angel would know. And imaginary friends were again in between.

The stunning result comes from the youngest children. "Do you know what's in this bag?"

"No."

"If I showed this bag to your best friend and nobody showed her what's inside, would your best friend know what's in the bag?"

"Yes."

Over and over, eighteen of the nineteen three-year-olds answered that their best friend would know. Unlike the matchbox test, the children never learned what was in the bag. And each child had just, seconds before, admitted not knowing the contents. In addition, all the three-year-olds said God, an angel, and their invisible friend would know the contents. Only one child said Santa would not know. Even all but three three-year-olds said a dog would know too.

At the end of the interview, we asked some of the more talkative kids how their best friend would know.

"They just would." "I don't know but they'll know."

"Can you see through the bag?"

"No."

"Could your friend see through it?"

"No."

"So how will they know?"

"It will be in their head, they'll know."

In other words, even under scrutiny, they insisted their friends would know. The closest to this result was in Malawi, where three-year-olds also attributed knowledge to humans at a high rate (70 percent); in Kenya the rate was 50 percent (and we didn't interview three-year-olds in Nepal or do the bag test in the US). The result from the Dominican three-year-olds, at 95 percent, is even more striking. I don't doubt that some children base what others know upon what they themselves know, as egocentrism predicts. But it is clear that something else is going on in many children, perhaps a deep bias towards assuming others have helpful information.

Gossip! Working over these results, I recalled a theory by the British psychologist Robin Dunbar, one based upon his studies of gossip. The gist of the theory is this: Humans, as deeply social animals, have benefited from group living. From food-sharing to group defense in the face of predators, social existence has served the species well. But it's not all easy. Some within the group take advantage of others; those are the bullies and jerks of a pack. Primates—human and otherwise—generate alliances to counteract or moderate the power of the bully. Think of the TV show *Survivor*, in which alliances are crucial. For most primates, these alliances are maintained and strengthened through grooming (hours and hours of picking nits and petting among chimps for example). Humans, according to Dunbar's research, spend an equivalent amount of time engaged in gossip. Gossip, here, is not so much the dubious-information or juicy-news variety, but more generally, gossip is talk about social stuff—who did what, who's in trouble, who is where, who knows what, who's in or out, and so on.

As Dunbar points out and the *Oxford English Dictionary* confirms, the term *gossip* originates from combining two Old English words: *god* (as in *God*) and *sibb* (as in *sibling*, but the term is broader, including any relative). A godsibb was a person, a godfather or godmother or baptismal sponsor, a relative in God. Later it came to mean a close person with whom one talks, and eventually it was used to describe the act of talking with that godsibb.

Sharing information, listening to news about friends and relatives, talk about who's hurting or celebrating, identifying problematic behavior, consulting others about our kids, sorting out who to trust and when. All this social talk, especially in face-to-face conversation, is the glue of alliances, generating trust and care in our relationships. Dunbar believes gossip is the human form of grooming, helping us keep track of one another, stabilizing our alliances, and maintaining our bonds. It could be, then, that when young children assume others know, they are reflecting a deep survival pattern in human existence: namely, that others, especially allies, have important information. I may not know what's inside the bag, but my best friend, invisible friend, angel, God, Ganesh, and sometimes even a chicken will know."

I thought, "What if invisible friends are godsibbs?"

In the land of Id, imaginary friends are rooted in early childhood confusion, compensation, and egocentrism. In a world of gossip, of godsibbs, imaginary friends are rooted in a deeply social mind thriving on companionship. As I reflect upon the results now, as I consider young children over and over insisting that others know things, as I think of Leah and Coda and a two-year-old girl who set me straight with "They're pretend," as I remember four-year-old Nathan keeping quiet about his additional pretend friends because they told him to, as I ponder children from Louisville to Nepal sharing imaginary friends with siblings and visible friends, as I meditate upon all the social play among children see-through and otherwise, as I look back, I see egocentrism as a ghost town.

If anything, young children seem to be other-centric, *eccentric*. The word derives from the Greek *ek* (out) plus *kentron* (center). Before the word meant "strange or unconventional," *eccentric* was used to describe astronomical observations, objects that did not have orbits around the earth. Those astronomical objects turned out to be all the planets and stars. Perhaps children are more like Copernicus, eccentric in thinking, appreciating that the planets do not revolve around them. I began to imagine the children I'd met as little astronomers, looking to the heavens in wonder. They know there is much more to the cosmos than can be seen in the daytime, even more than can been seen with the eye or telescope at night. Perhaps they know, if only intuitively, it takes imagination to see beyond ourselves.

PART III

Between Heaven and Earth

CHAPTER 9

ORIGINAL KNOWING

"Curiouser and curiouser!"

NOTEBOOK: "Dream, Guyacanes, DR. At some kind of auction—big outdoor space—like a flea market. I'm next to an old china cabinet, paneled in glass. I'm searching through the cabinet. I find a box—rectangular and small like a case for glasses. I open it and there's another one inside, and another and another. . . "

This dream came a couple of days after the last interview in the Dominican Republic, and I continue to reflect upon it. Exploring the world of invisible friends has been something like finding a glasses case inside another inside another inside another—as Kurt Vonnegut was fond of writing, "and so on." The world of invisibles is endless, multilayered, infinite, immeasurable, irreducible, and so on. I am charmed, once again, by the image of glass in this see-through realm, as well as the role of vision. A cabinet paneled with glass holds a case that itself holds glasses, those magical lenses through which those of us with aging eyes can see. *Vision.* An intriguing word, it can mean the ability to sense the world directly, with our eyes, maybe with the help of glasses. But it can also refer to dreams, revelations, or prophecies, from the mystic Julian's cataphatic visions to the Hopi Natalie's dream of her ancestors. Like a china cabinet made of wood and glass, there is something transparent and solid at work at the same time.

I set out on this adventure in a big open space of fascination with Crystal. I became curious about the overlap between imaginary friends and religion, with religious imagination. I opened a box and found shape-shifting friends and deities whose outer appearances—like the growing/shrinking Alice in a land of wonders—do not alter an inner essence. Proteus transforms from one figure to another, Jeff becomes Jeffette, God rejoices because "he is our Mother," Lucy shifts from the shape of a rabbit to a tiger. I soon discovered fluid boundaries between the living and the dead as well. Even in death the essence endures, whether Luo ancestors or Paw-Paw John, a resurrected god or invisible friend Stella who befriends an aunt who died. Beneath the essence is the relationship itself. Neither life nor death can separate us from love.

Inside another box, I noticed deep forms of sharing, from playing along with others and cooperation to sharing food and shekels in kib-butzim. Siblings share pretend worlds, places are set at the table for invisible friends, ancient gods are praised for food and drink, Jesus is known in bread, Malawian angels bring grain to children who would otherwise starve. What may have begun as a little tolerated scrounging or group hunting created the soil in which a deeply social mind could grow and bear fruit.

This led me to explore ways in which social cognition develops in children. From pointing and joint attention to gossip and theories of minds that sort out who knows what. Opening this theory-of-mind box, I found a way to compare and contrast the invisible minds of all kinds of agents in various parts of the world. God and Ganesh know what ordinary mortals do not. The Buddha and angels do too, along with Santa (for a while). Mayan elves, ancestors, fairies, and invisible friends are more likely to have special knowledge than people or dogs but not as likely as the gods. And there are always exceptions and variations, from culture to culture, religion to religion, household to household, child to child, even from one invisible friend to the next. Invisible Leah knows what's in the box but Coda does not, as we discovered in our very first interview.

And so on.

~~~~~~~~~~

What a turnaround. In one developmental picture, children are awash in fantasy so fully they do not know the difference between what's in their cabezas and what's in the world around them. In another, the one favored here, the sense-based world comes first and the imagination is a developmental achievement: the ability to dream possibilities, transform them, act as if one thing were another, play with mind stuff, transcend time and space as well as life and death, consider other perspectives, or to imagine there is a box inside a box inside a box.

While not every child has imaginary or invisible friends, I believe the phenomenon points to something fundamental about human knowing, its originality in the creaturely world, our original knowing. As strange as it may seem, DNA analyses comparing humans and chimpanzees find less than a 2 percent difference(depending upon the type of test), less than the difference between lions and tigers or rats and mice. Our biological differences from chimps are miniscule. They (and we) differ more from gorillas than we and chimps differ from each other.

But something happened between now and seven million years ago when our primate branches separated. While other great apes, and creatures generally, have all kinds of smarts in relation to each other and their environmental niches, nonetheless, human cognition explodes the scale. A few screeches and gestures have become a hieroglyphics, Spanish and Nepali, poetry, novels, histories, and a world full of libraries. An intuitive sense of more or less has become accounting, multiplication, calculus, engineering, and astrophysics. From simple stone tools to particle accelerators, from walking on two feet to flying planes and spaceships, from finding shelter in caves to building skyscrapers, the species has made the cognitive most of its slight biological difference.

In fact, as Michael Tomasello points out, the differences are so great they present a "time problem." Seven million years may sound like a lot of time, but frankly it's a blink of the biological eye. There hasn't been enough time for biological evolution and genetic variation to create each of the human cognitive capacities in all their complexities, from sophisticated tool-use industries and technologies to our complicated communication patterns and social institutions (think economic systems and governments). Something moved us cognitively out of the slow-developing time of biological evolution (where we still also live) and into the relatively rapid speed of historical-cultural time. With such a similar biological makeup as other great apes, the cognitive difference is likely very slight, but a tipping point all the same—some flap of a butterfly wing of difference that generated a whirlwind of change.

What is that change? My candidate is *imagination*. Wider than the sky, to paraphrase Emily Dickinson, deeper than the sea. The imagination unties us from the immediate, from the literal, from the narrow confines of things as they are. In turn, the imagination gives birth to historical-cultural time in the first place. We are able to consider events we have not directly experienced, times long before we were born. We can spin scenarios and consequences about the future as well, whether calculating the effects of using carbon-based fuels or spinning sci-fi yarns about millennia to come. Paradoxically, the imagination that allows us to think in historical-cultural time ultimately has led our species to appreciate the slow time of biological evolution as well as the deep time of geology and physics. The imagination allows us to consider origins themselves, a cosmos that began at some point in time, or better, initiated time in the first place. We can raise questions about those origins.

What was before time? Why is there a world at all? Is ours simply one of multiple universes—a cosmos in a cosmos in a cosmos? How or when or will it end? We can imagine our individual beginning and end as well as cosmic versions of the same. In short, we are able to wonder about life.

In Kenya I had a moment. Early in the stay, David and I went for a morning walk along a trail at the edge of the village where he was living. It was foggy in the distance, but he judged the sun was strong enough and the sky otherwise clear enough that the fog would burn off so that we could catch a glimpse of Lake Victoria. As we walked, I located the lake in the map of my mind. To that point it was the farthest south, globally, I'd ever been, and I asked David how far we were from the equator.

"Well, about ten kilometers from here there's a sign that marks the equator," he answered.

"Wow, that's close. So are we north or south of it?"

"Good question," he said, "the sign is due east from here. As far as I know, you could be in the southern hemisphere and I'm in the northern." Of course we were standing next to each other. He then pointed—the lake was in view. And we were quiet.

As the view absorbed my vision, my thoughts turned from geography to history, to prehistory to be more precise. I wondered how many generations had witnessed this view. We were standing in the heart of the Great Rift Valley after all, where the bones of our hominid ancestors go back millions of years. It is true that my more immediate ancestors migrated to the north sometime in the last twenty to forty thousand years and became *mzungus*, as they are called locally, white people. Even so, I felt a strong sense of all those earlier generations who had lived before us, as if they were standing there with me and my descendant, captivated by the view of a vast lake. And with David there, I began to wonder how many more generations would come. I could almost see them—past and future family—and wondered for a moment whether this was what having invisible friends felt like.

Here was a cloud of witnesses to earth's beauty taking me out of time, in a moment, and throwing me back into it all at once. Eons stretched out in the theater of my mind and I could see origins, endings, and a universe in between.

Two views characterize vision: the view from without and the view from within.

From without, our eyes take in wide horizons where earth and sky kiss, with trees and trails, lakes and clouds, colors and reflections and lights and shadows all embedded in a larger sense-scape full of sounds and smells and textures flooding a body weighted to the ground beneath our feet. Every waking moment. The environment offers an endless universe of stuff to be perceived.

From within, our minds can imagine the millions of years in a chain of life that formed bodies that can see anything at all. Here, within, Lucy, the three-million-year-old *Australopithecus* from Ethiopia is close kin, appearing as easily in the mind as a great grandmother I never met. In this view, the earth develops atmosphere, tectonic plates migrate across the globe crashing to create mountain ranges and continents. In the view from within, planets form and stars die and a universe that began with a bang some 14 billion years ago and could end in a whimper. Imagination. "O, what a world of unseen visions and heard silences," the great explorer of consciousness Julian Jaynes once wrote, "this insubstantial country of the mind! What ineffable essences, these touchless rememberings and unshowable reveries!"

But the view from within, this insubstantial country deeper than the sea, presents something of a Zen puzzle. Where is it? Or better, whence? From where do we stand to take in such a vast world? What trail do we trek to find a bird's-eye view of the Lake Victoria of our mind? The strangest thing of all about the imagination is that it isn't anywhere. As three-year-old Sarah offered, "George the monkey is nowhere!" Even a preschooler gets it. The view from within is a view from nowhere. At the same time, as we've learned from the children and their *nowhere* friends, see-through relationships matter. They offer companionship, dinner partners and homework buddies. Sometimes they have helpful superpowers, they may comfort or challenge as well as provide the shared joy of play. A remarkable fact of imaginary friends is that though they are nowhere, see-through, insubstantial, ineffable, touchless, and unshowable, they are relationships. At a time too easily characterized as childhood egocentrism, these relationships actually relativize children's egos with the presences offered in the unseen kingdom of the imagination. Invisible friends turn an *I* into a *We*.

Whether through crystalline characters or reveries about the origins of the universe, imagination throws the view from without into relief. Anything, everything is part of a larger setting. My individual view nests within a larger picture, continuously, as if there were a box inside a box inside a box inside a box. The imagination relativizes. I am a miniscule aspect of a never-ending realm. This likely explains why young children, as soon as they can speak in whole sentences, start asking why. Why is grass green, my hair black? Why are we going to the store now, why do strawberries taste good? And asking how. How does the car work? How do ants crawl up the tree without falling? How do clouds float?

Children are relentless questioners. While scrutinizing every inch of the world around them can drive parents a bit batty, the questions themselves would not arise without an imagination that appreciates that there is always a larger picture, a cause beneath an effect, a background that grants meaning to the foreground, as if all of life were an occluded-picture test. The figure in the cutout looks like a man watching television, but when the whole picture is revealed, we can see an elephant on a ball.

While the children we interviewed may have been tickled by discovering the whole picture, none of them were surprised—not even the three-year-olds—by the fact that a larger look could rearrange the meaning of the limited view. This was not magic to them; it was the way things are: anything, everything is nested. There is always more.

Here is what amazes me. Such an awareness of more does not seem to diminish the budding mind's sense of self or worth. If anything, being part of something larger buoys the young soul. Eight-year-old Natalie, the Hopi girl interviewed by Robert Coles, is strengthened in the face her grandmother's death as she dreams of meeting her ancestors on the mesa in an eternal circle. "That's when all the spirits will dance and dance, and the stars will dance, and the sun and the moon will dance, and the birds will swoop down and they'll dance, and all the people, everywhere, will stand up and dance." The grace of such a vision comes not by standing at the center of this circle but by seeing the circle of her own life, her grandmother's beginning and ending, her people's existence, and all creation itself in a cosmic dance. Natalie is relativized and vitalized, simultaneously, through a view from nowhere that connects her life to Life.

I believe the imagination is key to the cognitive differences between us and other primates, the explosion of knowledge in human beings. But not the imagination alone. At the heart of peculiarly human knowing is a *social imagination*. To overcome the time problem mentioned above, that which moves the species from strictly biological evolution and into cultural evolution, our ancestors had to find a way to hold onto the knowledge and practices from the previous generations and pass them on to the next. Sounds easy enough to us. We go to school, learn from our parents and friends, store information in books and computers, and employ experts to teach us how to write computer code, fix cars, or replace knees. We don't even need to learn individually each of these skills because we create societies and complex social institutions for pooling human knowledge and exchanging expertise and help. But that is now.

Imagine a couple of million years ago when the only cultural artifacts are simple stone tools, rock choppers that are hard to distinguish from a broken cobblestone. These early implements persist in the artifact record relatively unchanged for a million years. Presumably each generation, each group of hominids learned how to create and use these simple stone tools to crack open animal bones to yield the protein-rich marrow inside. Each generation learned to continue making and using these tools. No small feat. Other primates have been known to make discoveries and learn from each other (such as washing the sand off potatoes in a river or fishing termites from a mound). But these discoveries and practices tend to die out quickly, within a generation, until, say, another clever chimp rediscovers the benefit. Solving problems, insights, and perhaps even imaginative leaps are not unique to the human primate. But sustaining solutions, insights, and imaginative leaps over time, over generations, is. Other animals learn from each other; they engage in cultural learning. Humans accumulate cultural learning.

Our hominid ancestors sustained the practice of making stone choppers for a million years until they began shaping rocks into stone axes with sharp edges that could cut and slice and make scavenging easier or could even be thrown into a herd of grazing water buffalos in hopes of picking off a feast. Like the choppers before them, these axes persisted for generations, another million years, until an even greater diversity of tools appear. And greater, and greater. Each generation sustains the helpful know-how and eventually begins to tinker, improve, reimagine, and re-create the artifacts and practices from the earlier generations. In the twinkle of an evolutionary eye, we're building particle accelerators to smash electrons to better understand the creation of the universe.

The point is that humans can accumulate learning. The imagination of our species not only dreams and innovates, but it shares and stabilizes as well. Our creative, wild minds are nested within the context of shared knowing that builds upon and sustains learning.

A couple of clever experiments comparing human children with other great apes may help make the point more clearly. One is about learning and the other about teaching.

Learning. For all the talk about "aping" behaviors, the ways we imitate others, most apes are not so good at or interested in imitation. But human children are. In a revealing experiment led by Katherine Nagell, chimps and human two-year-olds try to obtain a prize (a toy for the kids, food for the chimps) through some fencing. They are given a rake to help. Older versions of such experiments found chimps to be quite talented at using such instruments to attain and scoop out-of-reach objects. But this experiment was different. The researchers demonstrated how to use the rake to get the prize. They did so using two different methods of holding the rake to see whether the method made a difference. The tool was not a typical garden rake. Its tines were long and far apart and the prize easily slipped through the spaces, making the process slow and frustrating. However, turned upside down, with the block that holds the teeth on the floor, the rake worked great. The researchers demonstrated the efficient method of raking to some chimps and the inefficient method to others. The demonstration made no difference—the chimps used the efficient method either way. They likely didn't even need the demonstration. But with the kids, the demonstration did matter. If shown the efficient method, children used it; shown the slow, teeth-side-down, arduous method, the two-year-old humans used the inefficient technique. Chimps cared about the task and used their problem-solving skills to rake in the prize with little fuss. Children focused upon the behavior of the demonstrator and imitated. They were so cued into the behavior of another that the efficiency of the method became secondary.

Of course human children, including two-year-olds, can also be good problem solvers and find efficient solutions to challenges—that is not the point here. The point is that the goal of gaining a prize (which they got whichever way they raked) was nested within a desire to share the intentions of others (to use the rake in a certain way). Such is a social mind, an ultrasocial cognition, the kind that can copy the behavior of others for a million years.

The other experiment contrasting human and nonhuman minds has to do with teaching—informing, showing, demonstrating, intentionally sharing knowledge. Accumulated cultural learning not only utilizes the kind of social mind that sustains knowledge over time, but it is powered by education. Teaching is the particle accelerator of cultural knowledge.

This experiment is much more complex than using rakes, but it too promises a prize to its subjects (two- and three-year-old children as well as mature chimps and orangutans). Three buckets are set before a subject. There is a curtain between the buckets and the subject; the curtain can be opened so that the subject can see the buckets or closed so that the subject cannot see them. While the curtain is closed, an experimenter places the prize (food or stickers) in just one of the buckets. All the child or chimp must do to win the prize is pick the correct bucket. A one-in-three chance. This is the game.

But in a follow-up round, when the curtain is opened back up, one of the two experimenters tilts the prize-containing bucket so that the subject gets a sneak peek. (She does this while the other experimenter looks away for a moment.) So this is the new game in which the subjects have a helper, and all subjects except one forgetful orangutan chose the right bucket.

In a third round, the same procedure is followed but this time the helper does not tilt the bucket and instead points to the correct one. Same game but with a different form of helping. All of the subjects—human and nonhuman—followed the point and looked at the prize-filled bucket. And all of the human children, in turn, chose the right one. But the nonhumans chose the correct bucket only a third of the time, at the same rate as chance.

In short, all subjects could read the intention of pointing; they understood that the experimenter wanted them to look at a particular bucket. But only human children comprehended the intention behind the intention of pointing—the intention to inform them. As the authors of the study put it, the nonhumans acted as if they thought, "There's a bucket. That's boring. Where's the food?" They did not understand the context of the pointing, the larger picture that revealed the intention behind the intention of pointing. The children understood immediately, intuitively, that the helper was sharing with them the intention to find the prize. That's what helpers do. But the chimps and orangutans apparently had no expectation of a helper, no expectation that another would intentionally inform them.

So, imagination alone is a necessary but insufficient means for a species to accumulate knowledge. Required is a social imagination cued into the ways and knowledge of others. Needed is a social imagination that not only learns and sustains learning over time, but one that that helps and informs and accelerates the accumulation of knowledge. The joint attention witnessed in a baby's pointing eventually creates a platform upon which a social imagination can stand. A ten-month-old holds up her pacifier for you not because she needs you to do something with it but for the sheer joy of sharing how great it is. "Look at this!" The fact that so many of the young children around the globe we interviewed were more likely than not to assume others would know things—even when those others were dogs and chickens and see-through friends—makes much more theory-of-mind sense in this context. Kids expect to learn from others.

As surely as the bodies of babies grow and thrive through physical feedings, young minds grow and thrive through a social imagination that shares views, provides information, and creates intentions behind intentions.

There is one more critical point regarding this social imagination. It makes cooperation possible. Even easy. In the world of primates, humans are the great cooperators. You may now think I have lost my invisible-friend-loving mind. A look at national news, global headlines, or even a three-year-old on a cranky morning might suggest otherwise. Agreed. Any of us can be intensely uncooperative. But as a species, we indeed belong to a different cognitive order when it comes to putting our heads together.

Something as simple as carrying a log with someone else doesn't happen among nonhuman primates (in the wild anyway). But humans not only share attention, they can share intentions—the desire and commitment to do something together. They create joint goals. To do so demands, again, the we-mode. To carry a log together, two people each subordinate and coordinate individual goals to the joint goal, *our* intention. We both have to know that we both are trying to do the same thing. If we share this intention, this goal, I can make adjustments in the way I hold the log in light of the way you hold it and vice versa; we can make adjustments to the pace; or we can decide to take a break when needed. Each of our wills is relativized to the joint commitment to move the log.

A striking aspect of this joint intention is that it too is born of the view from within, a view from nowhere. A joint intention requires that I mentally represent your role in a collaboration as well as my own all at the same time. In this invisible space, I can see you and I can see you seeing me, who is seeing me seeing you, in an infinite loop that should make us dizzy but does not in practice. The shared goal is the imaginative platform upon which we both stand to see ourselves and coordinate our roles. Humans are able to do this quite easily, even without consciously thinking about it. We play along with one another. But the ability to share an intention appears just out of intuitive cognitive reach for other great apes.

A cognitive caveat and moral note: our species-unique minds do not make us better than other primates, only different. In fact, the amazing power of our minds makes us dangerous—to ourselves, to other creatures, to the planet itself as our innovating minds cooperate in all manner of deadly ventures. Look again to the news. Sin and evil, in my moral-religious tradition, is less about breaking rules and more about the twisting of otherwise good gifts (like cooperation) for hurtful, hateful purposes. You and I can share hateful intentions. We can cooperate to achieve violent goals. As far as I can tell, this happens most often when we mistake the small cutouts in our view of the world for the full picture, substitute a part for the whole, regard the particular as the ultimate. My kind—race, ethnic group, nationality, species—is what matters above all else. My belief, philosophy, or religion represents ultimate truth. The mistake is to forget the nesting, to shut down the ways in which my view rests within an even greater one, reducing the more into less. Moral philosophers use various terms for expressing this twisted temptation in us: treating a *Thou* as an *It* as already considered, turning irreducible *mysteries* into mere *problems*, taming the *infinite* by *totalizing* or *absolutizing* the finite.

Our minds are the blessing and the curse of a species that shares views and intentions, sustains knowledge and behaviors over time, and cooperates. If people are indeed mysteries and not just problems, if life is characterized by the infinite in which there are boxes inside boxes, the moral task is to resist the voice of the serpent who says, "Eat this fruit and you (your ideas, kind, religion) will be like God—ultimate." Given the kind of minds we have, the moral task is to recognize the sense of the infinite value of others, of life itself.

Religious beliefs and practices at their worst amplify the voice of temptation: we have the total, infallible truth. Religion at its best cultivates the spirit of more, of mystery, of seeing through surfaces to the infinitely irreducible—the sacred. It does so not only by calling out evil, but more positively, by stoking wonder. Sharing a view characterized by the sense of the sacred—that others are a reflection of the holy, that reality is shot through with irreducible mystery—cultivates wonder. As Abraham Heschel puts it: "We do not wonder *at* things anymore; we wonder *with* all things." Considering the glory of reality, he says, is less about having a thought, but sharing in a thought, one in which we realize we are not alone. *Radical amazement* Heschel calls it, and it "refers to all of reality; not only to what we see, but also to the very act of seeing as well as to our own selves, to the selves that see and are amazed at their ability to see." Each act that reflects wonder fuels the fire of radical amazement. To treat another—say, a child in our care—as if she is irreducible is to nurse her on wonder. To be loved, as if my life too were sacred, is to experience a radically amazing reality in which I share.

To the extent that the power of our minds nests within a larger framework of wonder, our species may have a shot.

"Test one, two," I say on the recording. "Hang on a second. I'm going to put you on speaker." Cora had just called, excited, and wanted to tell me about something that happened to her the day before in Birmingham. She had traveled with a friend from her home in Nashville to Alabama in order to run in a kind of race I'd never heard of before—a microbrew race. Participants run or walk or bike from brewery to brewery, stop for a sample, and depending on the venue, have a bite to eat or play horseshoes or cornhole (similar to horseshoes but with bean bags). Being the first to cross the finish line has nothing to do with winning. Hanging out with friends, playing, and having a beer does. This race was not only for home brewers and young adults; Cora said families with kids were part of it too. It was more picnic than race or barhopping.

She wasn't two sentences into telling me the story when I stopped her and asked if I could record it. She agreed.

"So," she said, "I was at a brewery playing cornhole with my friend Claire, and this little girl came up, who was with her parents, and she asked if she could play cornhole with us. We played with her a while and when we were kind of done she said, 'Do you want to meet my horse Strawberry?' And we said, 'Yeah!' She was wearing a little backpack and I was expecting her to pull a toy out, but instead she runs to where her parents were, a little way away, and she starts petting an imaginary horse."

Cora explained that the little girl and family were close enough for Cora to hear. One of the parents says, "Oh, you're showing them Strawberry."

"Then," Cora continued, "she proceeded to show us how she rides Strawberry. With very detailed movements, she brought Strawberry out, as if pulling him by the mane. And then sat him down so she could lift one leg over and then got him to stand back up. Then she galloped off all around the outside of the brewery and she came back and dismounted Strawberry in the same careful way. Then she asked if we wanted to ride Strawberry. I said, 'Yeah, I do.' So I followed her lead and did the same thing she did to mount Strawberry. Lifted one leg up and put it over and then held on like I was ready to go."

Cora paused for a moment, gathering herself for the punch line. "She, the girl, looked at me and said, 'Um, you're riding him backwards.'"

Cora and I both howled.

After settling down, Cora continued the story. "'Oh, okay,' I said. I did the same thing she did to dismount and asked, 'Can you turn him around so that I can ride him in the right way?' So she did, with care, turn him around. I get back on and galloped off with Strawberry and came back and dismounted."

Cora told me that she then went over to talk to the parents. "I told them that I thought this was great because my dad does research on imaginary friends. They said, 'Oh, we've got more for you,' and told us that Strawberry was new. But they'd had Little Mouse around for a while, a couple years. Then they asked their daughter how she got Strawberry."

Cora said, "She told me her friend Little Mouse gave her a pretend watch for her fifth birthday. This pretend watch had a wishing-well button. So she used the wishing-well button to ask for a horse, and she named him Strawberry. And that was how she got Strawberry."

In the end, there is no end. Strawberry is born in the imagination of a child by way of an earlier imaginary mouse, who in turn gives a five-year-old a pretend watch, which itself has a wishing-well button. Who knows how deep that well is? On the surface, it's easy to reduce this to silliness, to magical thinking, but that's like riding Strawberry backwards. Better to dismount and try again. Something deep is going on. I see the ability to imagine more, the desire to play with others—sharing a view and friends—and a capacity to see through to a world within a world within a world, and so on. And they are all connected, held together with love and joy in the heart and mind of a young child who is discovering the irreducible, endless, more, sacred.

"Under the running sea of our theories and scientific explanations," Abraham Heschel writes, "lies the aboriginal abyss of radical amazement."

CHAPTER 10

FRIENDS OF GOD

*"Why is a raven like a writing-desk? . . . Have you
guessed the riddle yet?" the Hatter said, turning to
Alice again.*

*"No, I give it up," Alice replied. "What's the
answer?"*

"I haven't the slightest idea," said the Hatter.

A FRIEND OF MINE, Cláudio Carvalhaes, wrote what is likely the
most beautiful book I've never read. Published in his country of origin,
Brazil, it's written in Portuguese and called *Oi Pai* (Hi Dad). The sub-
title translates in English as *An Imaginary Conversation between a Son
and an Enchanted Father*. Cláudio was in graduate school in New York
when his father, in Sao Paulo, unexpectedly died. Soon afterwards, as
if to bridge the distance between the US and Brazil, as if to narrow the
gap between heaven and earth, Cláudio began a daily practice of going
to a favorite coffee shop, buying two cups—one for himself and one for
his father—and sitting at a table, holding long, imaginative conversations with his invisible, enchanted father. The book, he tells me, is full
of these talks, along with the poems, prayers, reflections, and songs that
emerged from them.

Peering into the glasses case of childhood imagination, I gained a glimpse into a kind of vision that sees through the surfaces of reality to invisible minds and more, the kind of mind that can hold meaningful conversations even through the distance of death. I have been struck by the relationships—as such—with invisible beings, relationships found across cultures. Children and adults alike form bonds with unseen figures, play or pray or talk with them, honor or engage them with rituals and art and music. The communities explored here are composed not only of relationships between people but of ties between the seen and unseen alike.

The historian of religion Robert Orsi argues that this "network of relationships between heaven and earth" is too often neglected by scholars of religion in favor of the beliefs and ideas for explaining reality. "I can think of no religious world," he says, "that does not offer practitioners opportunities to form deep ties with saints, ancestors, demons, gods, ghosts, and other special beings in whose company humans work on the world and on themselves." Reflecting upon these invisible beings alongside imaginary companions has led me to wonder whether children's see-through friends could be Celtic púcas like Harvey, saints who bounce with life, spirits of the dead who bring comfort to sad little girls, angels or translucent fairies, allies or godsibbs or Mayan spirits leading me about the Yucatán. Powers I only pretend to understand.

Through these encounters, I have become increasingly intrigued by the parallels between children with invisible friends and the way some novelists talk about their characters, just as Frederick Buechner *discovered* his main character, Leo Bebb, was a saint. I have writer friends who share similar stories. "Brad, it was like the characters became real and had minds of their own," Frank Rogers told me of the people in his novel *God of the Shattered Glass.* "They would even do things in the story that I did not intend, and even wish they wouldn't do," he said, "but they did them anyway." The main character, Tony, "would say things in a conflict, for example, and I would think to myself, 'Oh no, don't say that, you don't mean it,' but he would say it anyway. Heartbreaking. He wouldn't listen to me."

Novelist Karen Dionne in her blog tells a parallel story about her writing and the difference she has found between types of stories. She describes how her first two novels were plot-driven and how she crafted characters to the needs of the story. But, she explains in the blog, the next novel was different. "This time, the character came to me before the story, as I was searching for a backstory for the main character in a different novel. I woke up in the middle of the night, and this character was in my head talking to me, telling me her history and who she was. I wasn't dreaming about this character. She was just there, as real as if she were sitting in a chair beside me." Dionne goes on to say how the character never left. She was so persistent that Dionne decided the character needed her own story, one different from the one she had originally planned, one in which the writing became almost effortless. Dionne ends the piece with a pinch of metaphysical irony, saying, "I used to think that when writers said their characters spoke to them, they were anthropomorphizing the writing process. I realize now that's because my characters never talked to me before. Now that they've started, I hope they never stop!"

So prevalent is this experience, a research project at Durham University in England called Writers' Inner Voices is currently investigating the phenomenon. It points out the parallels between the way readers get to know characters through reading and the way authors get to know them through writing: "Just as through reading we feel we come to 'know' people who momentarily seem 'real,' many of the authors we interviewed spoke of the writing of characters not as a process of *creating* them but becoming acquainted with them." Writers were asked to describe the quality of what they "hear" when they write. Most struggled with an answer, saying things such as "It's like it's a silent voice, but it's not like I'm seeing text, so there's something going on. But it's not. I'm hearing it rather than seeing it, but I'm not actually hearing a definite loud voice. That's about the only way I can describe it." Somehow these voices are there and not there simultaneously. Or in the words of another writer: "This is very odd; in a weird kind of way . . . I'm saying I'm hearing a voice but I can't actually tell you what it sounds like." He continues, "If you pushed me on that I'd probably say it doesn't sound like anything, it doesn't actually sound like I'm hearing but I am hearing it." Much like the view from nowhere, the writing voice is inaudible but also "heard," invisible yet visible text. Paradoxes abound.

Essayist and novelist Roger Rosenblatt explores the process beyond fiction, in relation to all kinds of writing, if not any creative endeavor. He points out, first, that "the invisible world governs the visible like a hidden nation-state." From magnetic fields and electrical currents in the physical world to the desires, thoughts, passions, and tastes of our interior lives, invisibles rule. In writing too. "You come up with an image, phrase or sentence. Your head snaps back, and you say to yourself, Where did *that* come from?!" The entire writing-reading enterprise is loaded with unseen dynamics, not the least of which is writing for unseen readers, "who remain a secret, with secret lives." The whole relationship is unseen, he says. "We write to an invisible world on which we depend. If you happen to recognize yourself in someone or something we create, that's all good. But the writer will never know that, or you. You are Harvey, our invisible, six-foot (we hope, gentle) big-eared friend."

Susan Sontag caps the point as she too discusses both essay and fiction writing in her book *As Consciousness Is Harnessed to Flesh*, a collection of her notebooks and journal reflections. "I experience the writing as given to me," she says, "sometimes almost as dictated. I let it come, try not to interfere with it. I respect it, because it's me and yet more than me. It's personal and transpersonal, both." As with children and their imaginary friends, Sontag's reflections highlight the way in which the writer's imagination relativizes the sense of self without diminishing the author—*personal and transpersonal* at the same time. An I in relation to a Thou relationship creates a We.

One relaxed morning in Nepal, I found a breakfast place along the lake called Mike's Restaurant that served coffee American-diner style—free refills. Perhaps it was the caffeine, or maybe it was the ubiquitous temples and gods and goddesses about me, but in my journal I posed a metaphysical question to myself: "What if the IFs are real? In what sense could they be real? When a child's friend is Jesus or Buddha or the Holy Spirit, one is given pause to call them imaginary. When a child's world is populated with so many invisibles, we have to consider the possibility that they are real.Okay, what is real? Without a doubt, the relationships are real, and this is remarkable. It's as remarkable as forming relationships with a teddy bear, with a cartoon character, a superhero, or with a character in a novel or a movie."

What is real? Fictional characters who come to a novelist in the night? A late father sitting across the table in a coffee shop? Crystal and Quack-Quack? An invisible reader with whom a writer shares a world? For that matter, am I real? How about the Holy Spirit with whom a little boy prays and reads the Bible?

Without a doubt the relationships are real, and this is remarkable. I was led into these adventures with invisible friends not only by a fascination with a childhood mind that easily connects to invisible characters but also by the parallels with religious imaginations in children and adults alike. Inevitably the reality question arises: is God just another imaginary friend? The flipside of a mind that knows it can imagine, pretend, invent, and generate characters is that this is a mind that knows it can make things up or be wrong. Three-year-olds know their imaginary friends are pretend. By six, most of us understand that we can have false beliefs. While I am convinced by the loads of empirical research that Freud got early childhood wrong when it comes to the ability to distinguish fantasy from reality, nonetheless, he could still be right when it comes to the realm of gods and angels. "They're pretend!" In the territory of invisible powers and presences, there is no empirical test to help us sort out the ambiguities of see-through worlds and the characters who may live in them. In fact, the updated version of a psychological critique of religion rests less on the Freudian id but squarely on the kinds of cognitive research the IF project carried out: theory of mind. We saw how easily children attribute minds not only to mosquitoes and trees but to invisible spirits and gods. And we saw among young children how often those minds know in extraordinary, godlike ways. It is no large leap then to see the religious imagination as an extension of theory of mind written upon the blank page of the universe.

Evolutionary psychologist Jesse Bering even calls theory of mind the source of a *belief instinct*. He points to the 1956 film *The Red Balloon* to illustrate how hair-triggered theory of mind is. If you've never seen the film, a little boy, Pascal, discovers and retrieves a bright red helium balloon tied to a lamppost. Thrilled, Pascal takes the balloon everywhere. But when he arrives at home, the balloon is cast out the window by an unidentified but clearly grumpy adult. The balloon takes off into the air and floats about the building for a few moments. Then it descends back to the window where the boy can see the balloon and presumably the balloon sees the boy. At this point we know we are into a magical story since the balloon seems to have its own mind and wants to be with Pascal as much as the boy wants to be with the balloon. A friendship is born and the balloon accompanies Pascal wherever he goes, even when the boy isn't holding the string. Sadly, near the end of the film, a herd of cruel boys pops the balloon and we witness the death of a friendship.

But in a kind of resurrection scene, balloons from all over the city gather and find Pascal, eventually carrying him off into the sky.

This award-winning film works because our theory of mind easily attributes desires, personality, knowledge, and a soul even to a balloon. For Bering, God is a red balloon. The development of theory of mind was a powerful evolutionary cognitive tool that helped our hominid ancestors better predict and explain the behaviors of others. However, it worked too well and now has flooded our social brains. The result: "we overshoot our mental-state attributions to things that are, in reality, completely mindless." This includes the idea of God. "It may feel as if there is something grander out there . . . watching, knowing, caring. Perhaps even judging. But, in fact, that's just your overactive theory of mind. There is only the air you breathe." Like Freud a hundred years earlier, Bering believes it's time to rid ourselves of the God illusion. Pop!

I would not be in the work I'm in if I were as convinced as Bering of what he calls a *fact*. He may well be correct, that the gods are nothing but air, but I believe there are shortcomings in the argument that stand out: one is philosophical and the other is psychological.

First, it would have helped Bering's argument to have wrestled with a deeper philosophical question: Why is there something rather than nothing? On the surface, the question may seem like idle speculation, but under scrutiny, it persists as a never-ending puzzle. The brute fact of being, of somethingness, poses the question. Minds that can imagine an ever-larger context or a time before time or multiple universes are minds that can imagine the counterfactual of nothingness. The existence of a world certainly doesn't prove that there is a god or gods or creative power that intentionally gave rise to the cosmos; existence doesn't even mean that there is purpose or reason for life to be. But the suchness of life hovers outside the window of minds that can imagine.

Perhaps the better argument against a religious imagination is that our minds play a different trick on us. It's not so much that we project a mind onto the universe (in the form of a god) but that our minds can always imagine more, another box, the infinite. When we climb this eternal ladder as far as we can, either up or down, our minds assume there is some ultimate more—a god or Brahman or absolute unity or transcendence—that provides the final background to the foreground of the world. This too could be a way our original knowing tricks us into religious thinking in the face of somethingness.

Even so, the ongoing exploration of life does indeed find boxes within boxes, systems nested within other systems—from the air we breathe and subatomic particles to solar systems and galaxies. The universe appears irreducible in every direction. The factness of life examined with scientific methods of observation keeps yielding more. Again, there is no straight line from somethingness to God, but the religious imagination at least tries to account for the fact of life and its ultimate origin. To reject religion outright or reduce it to a psychological dynamic suffers without some wrestling with the suchness of the world.

I believe there is another issue, psychological in this case, that makes reducing God to an overactive theory of mind too easy: doubts. Indeed, it could be the case that religious realities are illusions. But it's not as if religious people don't realize this. Most grapple with their doubts, skepticism, and unbelief. Our minds may be overactive theory-of-mind generators throwing souls into anything and everything wherever we go, but they are also characterized by unbelief and doubt, even among religious believers. If theory of mind creates a belief instinct, theory of doubt generates an unbelief instinct. If theory of mind flings souls everywhere and senses the gods against a blank slate of the cosmos, theory of doubt questions it all. Perhaps the popping of the God balloon is born of an overactive false-belief generator that too easily assumes others have bad information.

I come from a theological tradition that does not hide from the doubts and suspicions that our hearts and minds may house. In fact, like good science that considers any finding contingent, subject to further investigation, a healthy skepticism about our claims—theological or oth-erwise—helps us reconsider bad ideas and hurtful beliefs and may open possibilities for reformation and transformation. Even so, there are forms of doubt and skepticism that are existential, that can undermine the whole religious enterprise. And religious hearts and minds are not immune to this power. Theologian Edward Farley calls it the "nasty suspicion" that haunts theology itself: "Could it be that there are no realities at all behind the language of this historical faith? . . . Are Christian theologians like stockbrokers who distribute stock certificates on a nonexistent corpora-tion?" Eating forbidden fruit from the tree of knowledge seems to have opened our eyes to the ambiguities of existence: we know we can delude ourselves, we realize that to live is to die, we thrive on meaning that itself is contingent and fragile. Original knowing subjects our beliefs and our lives to a larger perspective, one that could reveal that we have it all wrong, that there is ultimately nothing rather than something.

The twentieth-century theological giant Paul Tillich describes the ways in which doubt and meaninglessness plague any existence, not only those of believers. Yet, he finds the potential in the life of faith a *courage to be* even in the face of doubt and anxieties rooted in the fear of mean-inglessness. This courage is not so much of the type that a heroic knight facing a fire-breathing dragon might possess, one mustered from within. The courage to be is larger than the I; it flows from the awareness that "one is accepted by that which infinitely transcends one's individual self." Such courage includes but is more than an individual capacity; it is born from a sense that the ultimate ground of life affirms our life. And just as courage is not the absence of fear but the ability to act despite fear, the courage to be is not the absence of doubt or meaninglessness but the affirmation of life that is bigger than death and despair, bigger than nothingness. This courage, says Tillich, is seen in "the paradoxical character of every prayer, of speaking to somebody to whom you cannot speak because he is not 'somebody,' of asking somebody of whom you cannot ask anything because he gives or gives not before you ask, of saying 'thou' to somebody who is nearer to the I than the I is to itself."

But doubt and unbelief are not only the purview of liberal theological traditions, they are just as much at work in more conservative or evangelical traditions. Stanford anthropologist Tanya Luhrmann has documented the challenge of believing in an invisible god by living among and worshipping with evangelical Christians both as a social scientific observer and as a participant. She too points out how an evolutionary account that points to hyperactive theory of mind leaves out part of the puzzle: it "does not explain how God *remains* real for modern doubters." She has studied carefully the ways Christians doubt, those who "find it hard to believe in an invisible being—let alone an invisible being who is entirely good and overwhelmingly powerful. Many Christians struggle, at one point or another, with the despair that it all might be a sham." While this may seem to be a peculiar challenge of modernity and the rise of scientific methods and enlightenment sensibilities, Luhrmann reminds us how the fourth-century Augustine agonized, how the eleventh-century Anselm despaired. "The long tradition of spiritual literature is full of intense uncertainty about the true nature of a being that can be neither seen nor heard in the ordinary way." So despite stereotypes of naïve believers resting upon unshakeable faith, religious beliefs and the ways of life that accompany faith are loaded with struggle. In the realm of invisibles, the sense of presence can be easily plagued by the sense of absence.

Luhrmann records the many expressions of this struggle in individual Christians she interviewed, as well as some of the practices used to help the faithful cultivate stronger relationships with an invisible God. At the Chicago Vineyard Church she participated in, the pastor encouraged people to treat God like a friend. Though she says he never used the term *imaginary*, "he invited us to behave with God the way children behave with imaginary friends." One of the ways of doing so was with a cup of coffee for God in the morning—to set out "an actual cup of steaming coffee, to place it on an actual table, and to sit down at that table with our own mug to talk to God about the things on our minds."

Like Cláudio with his father, like children with imaginary friends, the advice speaks to the power of relationship as well as the challenge of maintaining relationships haunted by invisibility. There is an as-if quality to the encounters—as if my enchanted father were sitting here, as if Baby Bear goes to school with me, as if the source of love and creation were at table in my kitchen. The as-if quality may be the best our original minds can do, given the ambiguities of presence and absence, views without and views within. But in all these situations, the as-if ultimately serves relationship, friendship, love.

Cláudio was kind enough to send a follow-up conversation he had with his father, ten years after his death, a portion of which I share. It was Father's Day, and after many years of disappointment for my friend because he was not able to become a father himself, a new opportunity emerged. He was about to marry a mother of three children, children who'd lost their father to cancer a few years earlier.

Hi Dad,

It's been so long since we spoke. What I feared the most is indeed happening, and I'm forgetting our memories. The memory and your presence do not decrease but are going other places inside of me. A tree is tattooed on my back to remind me of you in the seven layers of my skin and the walls of my heart. . . .

Despite all this, it seems that today I have a new opportunity. After losing so many possibilities, I'm becoming a father. And a mixture of fear and immense joy, expectation and terror, everything becomes feelings that pulse in all my pores.

Though he had always imagined that his children would be born to him, Cláudio realized the joy of parenting would not derive from being a birth father but by the life *shared with others*. He goes on to tell his dad of the ways this shared life was emerging, the ways in which he was already becoming a father to each of the children. Slowly, carefully, with love and fear and many challenges but moments of connection too: a kiss on the forehead from one child, words of love from another, tears flowing from the third when Cláudio was delayed for a visit.

That's how Dad, in all forms and ways, I am becoming a father. Slowly. All new, all difficult, all wonderful, all full of ups and downs. My guideline and direction, my compass and map in this whole endeavor has been the love with which I was loved by you. . . . Stay with me and help me, walk with me and help me become what you did so well: be a wonderful father.

Even through time, ups and downs, disappointments and new opportunities, and through death and the threats of nothingness, *without a doubt the relationships are real, and this is remarkable.*

Luhrmann says that after all the Sunday-morning gatherings and instructions in the Chicago Vineyard congregation, she scrawled in her notebook, in all caps "GOD IS YOUR BEST FRIEND." As I reflect upon her research, I think of the humble seventeenth-century French monk known only as Brother Lawrence, who describes his spiritual life as one in which he continually "practices the presence of God." In a series of letters to a friend, he describes applying his mind continually to God, "whom I considered always as *with* me, often as *in* me." He describes the practice as a simple attention and a habitual silent conversation between his soul and its creator. Like Cláudio becoming a father, this happens over time, slowly, carefully, with ups and downs and challenges. But the relationship becomes increasingly real through practice, even as it maintains an imaginative, as-if character. In his eighties, Brother Lawrence writes that this friendship with God is so full: "The time of business does not with me differ from the time of prayer; and in the noise and clatter of my kitchen, while several persons are at the same time calling for different things, I possess God in as great tranquility as if I were upon my knees at the blessed sacrament."

I think of Marco in the Dominican Republic, whose best friend, he said, is God. His invisible, but not imaginary, friend is Jesus Christ. I again think of Hwan, whose invisible friend is the Holy Spirit. I wonder, Will one of these children become the next Brother Lawrence? Or in the face of the doubts and questions that will inevitably come, will their closeness with the divine fade like a worn stuffed animal?

The question remains: Is God just another imaginary friend? Maybe. The overlap between invisible friends and religion intensifies the question. Given the ambiguities of life and death, given worlds visible and invisible, given theory of mind and doubt, given the suchness of the cosmos and its unobservable source, given all this, questions concerning the reality status of imaginary friends and invisible gods, ancestors, and angels will endure.

Imaginary friends and God have this in common: they are invisible relationships and bear the fruits that community and friendship bring. But here is one difference between the two types of invisibles: cultivating friendship with God is motivated not only by companionship but by a relationship with life itself, with its source, with the origin of all community. Friendship with God traces the love we have known from caring parents alive or dead to an ultimate source, sets the love known in the joy and challenge of new relationships against the backdrop of ultimate joy. Friendship with God is relationship with the well of all love, even a love made manifest in a child's imaginary friendship.

In Nepal I had a dream. Someone was giving a speech in my school's chapel and riffing on the word *relative*. The word can be a noun—aunts and grandparents are relatives, family relationships. The word can be an adjective—relative clauses in language, relative keys in music. Each is in relation to something else. In verb form we get *relativize*—to compare one thing to another. The dream speaker points out that we often use the term *relativize* to diminish the power of a claim; for example, the presence of multiple religions relativizes my religion. (I was dreaming in a country of many deities after all.) "But," the speaker pointed out, "we relativize our own lives when we get married or have a child or make a new friend. We are putting our lives in relation to more than ourselves—we relativize ourselves." The speech, or maybe it was a sermon, ended with a question: "Would God do the same?"

I woke up, fixed a cup of coffee and wrote my dream. As I finished writing, I realized that children are doing the same—relativizing themselves—with their see-through friends. But pondering the dream question—Would God do the same?—my thoughts took me to Israel, to the city of Safed in the northern part of Galilee. Two years earlier, I had co-led a travel seminar and we visited the city and its many synagogues. At an altitude of over a half mile, Safed sits at the highest point in the region and was the chilliest destination of our trip. Instead of the traditional yarmulke (skullcap), many of the thickly bearded men of the city wore wool stocking hats to cover their heads. I was happy to join them in this practice and grateful that I'd been letting my beard grow. More significantly, Safed is key to a tradition of Jewish mysticism, Kabbalah, because it was the home of the great sixteenth-century rabbi Isaac Luria, affectionately called the Ari (Holy Lion). He is said to have had regular visions of and long conversations with the biblical prophet Elijah.

As our guide led us through the Ari Ashkenazi Synagogue dedicated to Luria, he shared stories of the Ari's visions, and it was clear that in this place the walls between the living and the dead were as see-through as in a crystal palace. Luria and his community developed very precise practices for communing with the dead, *yihudim*, specifically for communing with the soul of a righteous person (tsaddiq) in order to gain wisdom and guidance for living. Often this communing took place at grave sites.

At this point on our trip, I had already conducted the Louisville study, so it was impossible for me not to consider the parallels between children's conversations with transparent companions and adults consulting ancient figures for wisdom. One realm may be playful, the other more serious, but the capacity to be in relationship with invisible others underlies both. The guide pointed to a corner in the ceiling and told us of a worshiper's more recent vision not of Elijah, but Luria himself. I was left with the impression that the Holy Lion was never too far away, hovering, filling the chilly air with his sacred presence. I could almost see him myself.

With my body in Nepal and mind in Safed, I thought of an ancient rabbinical idea: *tsimtsum*, or "withdrawal," a concept Luria drew upon in much of his teaching. "Tsimtsum relativizes God," I realized.

If you don't know the idea yet the word sounds vaguely familiar, you may have read Yann Martel's *Life of Pi* or seen the film based upon it. Tsimtsum is the name of the cargo ship the main characters take to emigrate from India. Ancient rabbinical writings used the concept to navigate the thorny theological issue of God's presence and absence. How could God be everywhere, yet particularly present in the Ark of the Covenant (with the commandments) or in the Jerusalem Temple's Holy of Holies? The answer is that God withdraws the Holy Presence from everywhere and concentrates it in these particular places.

But Luria, using the full powers of a religious imagination, took the concept much further, using tsimtsum to describe the origins of the cosmos itself. Before creation, there is only God. The Holy Presence is all that exists, is *All in All*. There is nowhere or nothing or no being that is not God. To make room for a world other than this presence, the Holy All contracts within itself, leaving a free space, a vacuum, a realm that is not God, which is nonetheless ringed by the divine presence: a nothing necessary for a new something. God then reaches into this emptiness with divine light and forms ten vessels within the otherwise Godless realm, much as the hand of a potter forms a bowl on the empty surface of a wheel. These vessels are the beginning of creation, the substance of a universe that is not God but created and loved by the Divine. Thus, by making room within the All in All presence, God is relativized by creation. The world and all therein is God's and born of a desire to be in relation, imagined into being. Oneness becomes multiple. I thought again about children relativizing themselves with imaginary friends. "Are we God's imaginary friends?," I wondered.

It was only a few days later that I saw the Himalayas towering above the city. One peak in particular rose above the rest like the dorsal fin on a shark. Mount Machhapuchare it is called locally, Fish Tail. The peak is off-limits to climbers because it is considered sacred, the home of the god Shiva. While Shiva is generally a destroyer, he can create as well. As a man in the Fish Tail Bookstore explained it to me, when the god of love, Kamadeva, tried to shoot Shiva with his arrows of passion, Shiva burned the god to ashes. Shiva destroys. But later, out of love for his wife Parvati, Shiva brings Kamadeva back to life again. Destroying death, Shiva creates.

It seems that whether in the hills of Safed or along the peaks of the Himalayas, the driving force of creation is a relativizing love.

In Luria's vision, some of the vessels formed with the light of God were not stable and they shattered. Creating and destroying are never too far apart. Something about the act of creating is unstable, open to the unexpected, even for God in this account. God goes about mending (*tiqqun*) the damage, and the result is the good creation we read about in Genesis, the paradise inhabited by Adam and Eve. But, as the story goes, paradise is lost again, reshattered, when the first couple eat the forbidden fruit, recapitulating the original shattering of the vessels. The transgression throws creation off its potter's-wheel balance. The eyes of the couple are open to the instability of creation, of life plagued by the nothingness of destruction and death. And so it is for all of us since.

But just as human existence replicates the divine shattering, so too it can go about tiqqun, mending creation. Mending is the ultimate meaning of existence in this tradition. The purpose of all righteous deeds, religious practices, and love itself is to regather the light from the broken vessels of earth. Here, each and every individual act of repair reaches beyond itself and into the ultimate repair of the cosmos. Each act of kindness—tending the brokenhearted, extending hospitality, rebuilding crumbled lives, creating peace treaties, mending communities, respecting self and others, and more—helps reorganize the divine light and repair the world.

In this tradition God relativizes the Divine All to be in relationship with that which is other than God. Why? Love. This is the nature of divine pathos. Creation reflects the desire of the Creator, a love that imagined beyond itself. The cosmos and all the characters therein are imagined into being by the Holy Author.

Is God real? Proof is an empirical challenge in the world of invisibles. Could God be just another imaginary friend? Maybe. Yet, as I look by the light of this tradition, the questions flip. We are God's imaginary friends, along with all of creation, and that's what makes us real.

POSTSCRIPT

"Wake up, Alice dear!" said her sister; "Why, what a long sleep you've had!"

"Oh, I've had such a curious dream!" said Alice, and she told her sister, as well as she could remember them, all these strange Adventures of hers that you have just been reading about.

CORA, NOW LIVING IN CHICAGO, was home as I neared completion of this manuscript. We went for a run and she was kind enough to listen to me talk about original knowing and coffee friends and philosophical questions about somethingness as well as Jewish mysticism. Rounding the last corner into our neighborhood, I thanked her for listening, then asked, "So how should I end the book. Any last lines you can think of?"

She was silent while she considered the question. Finally she offered, "I don't know, but I'll ask Crystal." I smiled, and we both went quiet as we arrived home.

Later, as we talked about it, we each admitted the hope of getting an answer. One came, but not in the inaudible whispers of the mind I've come to expect from authors or children. Whether or not it was Crystal, I cannot say for sure, but an answer emerged in our conversation: *Vaya con Dios*. Go with God.

ACKNOWLEDGMENTS

I am grateful to so many—visible and invisible alike—who made this labor of love possible. First of all, thank you to Cora, whose rich imagination caught my attention once upon a time on the shores of Lake Winnebago. Likewise, thank you to all the children and their parents who granted me the privilege of interviewing them. Thank you to all those who helped arrange and conduct those interviews, beginning with my son and daughter-in-law in Kenya, David Wigger and Amy Wadsworth—and to their daughter, Elly, who showed up in a dream with a new language! (See chapter 4.) Thank you to Katrina Paxson, Lacey Ryan, Ada Asenjo, Jannine Sayago-Gonzalez, Fletcher Podoko, Owaga Ochieng, Bina Silwal, Emily Burdett, Oguda Ochieng, Pramod Karki, MacDonald Sandram, Effy Chalandwendo, Claire Willey Sthapit, and Jo Ella Holman. Thank you to Frank Rogers and Cláudio Carvalhaes for sharing their writing lives and characters so freely. I'm grateful to the gang at Hogwarts (Oxford) for our time together sweating over statistical methods and project ideas under the encouraging leadership of Justin Barrett, Emma Cohen, Miguel Farias, and Tenelle Porter.

The time at the University of Oxford with the Cognition, Religion and Theology Project, as well as all the research represented in this book, would not have been possible without funding from the John Templeton Foundation. They want you to know that the views expressed here are not necessarily those of the project, the university, or the foundation. I'm also grateful to Louisville Presbyterian Theological Seminary—its board of trustees and my colleagues—for their enthusiastic support and trust as I pursued this line of research, especially when its theological significance was anything but self-evident at the beginning. "You're studying what, Brad?"

I'm grateful to Allan Cole and to those participating in the Children, Youth, Church, and Culture seminar where I first presented some of the IF interviews. That presentation was subsequently published as "See-through Knowing: Learning from Children and Their Invisible Friends" in *The Journal of Childhood and Religion* 2, no. 3 (May 2011): 1–34. Portions of the journal article have been used with permission from the journal.

I'm grateful to Jane Larsen-Wigger and Richard Curtis, early readers of the manuscript, for their editing advice. And thank you to the great crew at Stanford University Press: Emily-Jane Cohen, Faith Wilson Stein, Tanya Luhrmann, Jessica Ling, Barbara Armentrout, and Ann Taves. It's been a pleasure working with you. As I told Cora, "Crystal's going to Stanford!" Thanks for giving her story a home.

APPENDIX

MAJOR STUDIES OF IMAGINARY
COMPANION PREVALENCE

STUDY	LOCATION	AGES	% IFS	WHOM INTERVIEWED	TIME FRAME	TOYS?
Harvey, 1918	US	Childhood	6%	Adults remembering	Ever	No
Hurlock & Burnstein, 1932	US	Childhood	28%	High school & college	Ever	Unclear
Svendsen, 1934	US	3–16	13%	Children	Ever	No
Ames & Learned, 1946	US	3–10	21%	Parents and observation of children	Ever and Present	Yes
Manosevitz et al., 1973	US	4	28%	Parents	Recently	Yes
Singer & Singer, 1990	US	Preschool	65% 55%	Children Parents	Present	Yes
Taylor & Carlson, 1997	US	3–4	28% 13% 40%	Child/parent agreement Parents	Present	Yes No Yes
Bouldin & Pratt, 1999	Australia	3–9.5	7% 17%	Parents	Present Ever	Unclear
Taylor, 1999	US	6–7	46% 27%	Children	After 4	Yes No
Pearson et al., 2001	UK	5–12	28% 46%	Children	Present Ever	No
Hoff, 2005	Sweden	10	52%	Children	Ever	Yes
Motoshima et al., 2014	Japan	3	49% 5%	Mothers	Present	Yes No
Lin et al., 2016	China	5–6	34% 7.5%	Child/mother agreement	Ever	Yes No
Giménez-Dasí et al., 2016	Spain	4–6	21%	Parents	Present	Yes
Wigger, 2018	Kenya	3–8 (5–8)	21% (19%)	Children	Present	No
	Malawi	3–8 (5–8)	23% (22%)			
	Nepal	5–8	5%			
	DR	3–8 (5–8)	34% (44%)			

Major Studies of Imaginary Companion Prevalence

ANNOTATED NOTES FOR APPENDIX

Each study was published in a book or peer-reviewed journal. Where possible, the terminology for an IF (e.g., invisible friend, imaginary companion) used by the study itself is provided.

Nathan Harvey, *Imaginary Playmates and Other Mental Phenomena of Children* (Ypsilanti, MI: State Normal College, 1918). Harvey estimates about 6 percent of children have had an imaginary playmate. It is not entirely clear what he bases this on, but his examples are all from adults remembering back, so they exclude those who may not remember having one.

E. B. Hurlock and M. Burnstein, "The Imaginary Playmate: A Questionnaire Study," *Journal of Genetic Psychology* 41 (1932): 380–92. The study administered a questionnaire to 701 high school and college students remembering back to childhood. There is no mention of toys or stuffed animals, only "Did you ever have an imaginary playmate?" Rate for women was 31 percent; men, 23 percent. Some figures were based on dreams or storybook characters.

Margaret Svendsen, "Children's Imaginary Companions," *Archives of Neurology and Psychiatry* 32 (1934): 985–99. Svendsen found 13 percent of children between three and sixteen years old had "invisible characters," and she explicitly excluded personified objects. Older children might or might not remember.

Louise Bates Ames and Janet Learned, "Imaginary Companions and Related Phenomena," *Journal of Genetic Psychology* 69 (1946): 147–67. Ames and Learned created a mixed sample by interviewing parents but also observing children in a nursery setting. They included not only imaginary companions but toys and impersonation of animals or others, as well as "general imaginative play," and found instances of one or more of these in 21 percent of the children.

Martin Manosevitz, Norman M. Prentice, and Frances Wilson, "Individual and Family Correlates of Imaginary Companions in Preschool Children," *Developmental Psychology* 9 (1973): 72–79. The team surveyed parents and found that 28 percent of four-year-olds had or had recently had an imaginary companion.

Dorothy G. Singer and Jerome L. Singer, *The House of Make-Believe: Children's Play and Developing Imagination* (Cambridge, MA: Harvard University Press, 1990). The Singers found 55 percent of US parents of "preschoolers" (exact age unclear) responding that their child had an imaginary playmate. They included stuffed animals and toys if the child endowed them with humanlike properties but not if the child simply carried them around. Even more children claimed one (65 percent), suggesting some children had one their parents did not know about.

Marjorie Taylor and Stephanie M. Carlson, "The Relation between Individual Differences in Fantasy and Theory of Mind," *Child Development* 68 (1997): 436–55. Taylor and Carlson found that 28 percent of US three- and four-year-olds had imaginary companions when relying upon agreement between parent and child. The figure is higher (40 percent) when relying on parents alone, due to the fact that several of the children did not confirm having one. Of the sample of all children, 13 percent reported companions that were invisible.

Paula Bouldin and Chris Pratt, "Characteristics of Preschool and School-age Children with Imaginary Companions," *Journal of Genetic Psychology* 160 (1999): 397–410. Bouldin and Pratt surveyed Australian parents, asking whether their children ever had a "vivid character" that they played with (17 percent said they did).

Marjorie Taylor, *Imaginary Companions and the Children Who Create Them* (New York: Oxford University Press, 1999). Taylor followed up with many of the children (only) in the 1997 study, with the children then being six and seven years old. Of the children who had not had an imaginary companion at three or four, 46 percent had developed one afterwards, with 81 percent of these being invisible (27 percent of the total sample). Taking the two studies together, 63 percent of the children (up to seven) had an imaginary companion at some point, with 43 percent of all the children (with and without imaginary companions) being invisible, not based upon a personified toy.

David Pearson, Helen Rouse, C. Doswell, C. Ainsworth, O. Dawson, K. Simms, and J. Faulconbridge, "Prevalence of Imaginary Companions in a Normal Child Population," *Child: Care, Health & Development* 27 (2001): 13–22. This is the largest study of its kind. Nearly 1,800 children were interviewed in the UK, ages five to twelve. The researchers used two phrases in the same question: "a friend nobody else can see" and "imaginary companion." The study found 28 percent of the children reported having an imaginary friend at the time of the interview, with the highest percentage being among six-year-olds (43 percent). Another 18 percent of the children in this study reported that they had previously had an imaginary friend (46 percent of total).

Eva V. Hoff, "Imaginary Companions, Creativity, and Self-image in Middle Childhood," *Creativity Research Journal* 17 (2005): 167–80. Hoff found 52 percent of the ten-year-old Swedish children she interviewed had or had previously had a "pretend playmate."

Yuko Motoshima, Ikuko Shinohara, Naoya Todo, Yusuke Moriguchi, "Parental Behaviour and Children's Creation of Imaginary Companions: A Longitudinal Study," *European Journal of Developmental Psychology* 11, no. 6 (2014): 716–27. Based upon interviews with mothers, Motoshima et al. found that eighteen of thirty-seven (49 percent) Japanese three-year-olds had imaginary companions, but only two of them (5 percent) were invisible.

Qiyi Lin, Hong Fu, Yingjia Wan, Nan Zhou, and Hui Xu, "Chinese Children's Imaginary Companions: Relations with Peer Relationships and Social Competence," *International Journal of Psychology* (2016), https://doi.org/10.1002/ijop.12392. In their study of five- and six-year-olds in China, Lin et al. relied upon agreement between child and mother. They differentiated invisible imaginary companions from personified objects and found 34.3 percent of children had or had formerly had one or the other or both. But only 7.5 percent of the total number had ones not based upon objects.

Marta Giménez-Dasí, Francisco Pons, and Patrick K. Bender, "Imaginary Companions, Theory of Mind and Emotion Understanding in Young Children," *European Early Childhood Education Research Journal* 24, no. 2 (2016): 186–97. Giménez-Dasí et al. surveyed parents in Spain and found 21 percent claimed their child had an imaginary companion at the time of the survey.

J. Bradley Wigger, "Invisible Friends across Four Countries: Kenya, Malawi, Nepal, and the Dominican Republic," *International Journal of Psychology* 53, no. S1 (October 2018): 46–52. Wigger interviewed children in four countries and found various rates. Children were three to eight years old, except in Nepal, where they were five to eight years old. Rates varied depending upon the age grouping.

NOTES

Introduction: See-through Knowing

Epigraphs: The quotes that preface each chapter are from Lewis Carroll. **Earliest study:** Clara Vostrovsky, "A Study of Imaginary Companions," *Education* 15, (March, 1895): 383–98; quote from 383. At the end of the article is a note by her colleague Earl Barnes, who apparently collected and published some of the material initially. Vostrovsky supplemented his material with her own. **Earliest book:** Nathan A. Harvey, *Imaginary Playmates and Other Mental Phenomena of Children* (Ypsilanti, MI: State Normal College, 1918); quote from 7. **Best book:** Marjorie M. Taylor, *Imaginary Companions and the Children Who Create Them* (New York: Oxford University Press, 1999). In addition, a very helpful introduction to the history of research into imaginary companions is E. Klausen and R. Passmano, "Pretend Companions (Imaginary Playmates): The Emergence of a Field," *Journal of Genetic Psychology* 167 (2007): 349–64. **"Lived by powers":** W. H. Auden, "In Memory of Ernst Toller," *Collected Poems* (New York: Vintage, 1991), 249.

Chapter 1: Life-Givers

"Pretend friends": Nathan's phrase "pretend friends" raises the issue of terminology for this phenomenon, for which there is great variability—among children and parents themselves as well as in the literature over the past century (see Appendix). Rather than trying to neaten this variability, I have chosen to reflect it by using various terms, including the simple abbreviation IF, which can stand for *invisible friend* or *imaginary friend*. **Research team:** I am very grateful to Ada Asenjo, Katrina Paxson, Lacey Ryan, and Jannine Sayago-Gonzalez—the interview team who helped recruit children to interview as well as helped to interview them (and record the sessions so that I could watch or listen later). **Ethical standards:** The project was reviewed and approved by the Institutional Review Board of Louisville Presbyterian Theological Seminary. Parents or guardians provided informed consent for any interviews conducted; children too provided verbal assent for interviews and use of the drawings. **Taylor quotes:** Taylor, *Imaginary Companions*, 23, 33. **Historical estimates of IF prevalence: Harvey, *Imaginary Playmates*, 24; Dorothy G. Singer and Jerome L. Singer *The House of Make-Believe: Children's Play and Developing Imagination* (Cambridge, MA: Harvard University Press, 1990), 99. **Prevalence across cultures:** See J. Bradley Wigger, "Invisible Friends across Four Countries: Kenya, Malawi, Nepal, and the Dominican Republic," *International Journal of Psychology* 53, no. S1 (October 2018): 46–52. **Milne quotes:** A. A. Milne and E. H. Shepard (illustrator), *Winnie-the-Pooh* (London: Methuen, 1926), 1. **Most studies count a toy:** Singer and Singer, *House of Make-Believe*, set this standard. **Jung quotes:** Carl G. Jung, *Memories, Dreams, Reflections* (New York: Vintage), 181, 183. **Leo Bebb character:** Frederick Buechner, "Faith in Fiction," in *Going on Faith: Writing as a Spiritual Quest*, ed. William Zinsser (Eugene, OR: Wipf and Stock), 43–64; quotes from 56–57.

Chapter 2: Flexibility

L'Engle quotes: Madeleine L'Engle, *A Wrinkle in Time* (New York: Farrar, Straus and Giroux, 1962), 64, 84. **Piaget and time:** Jean Piaget, *The Child's Conception of Time*, trans. A. J. Pomerans (New York: Basic Books, 1969), ix, ch. 1. **Transitional attachments:** See D. W. Winnicott, "Transitional Objects and Transitional Phenomenon," *International Journal of Psychoanalysis* 34 (1953): 89–97. **Coles interview with Natalie:** Robert Coles, *The Spiritual Life of Children* (Boston: Houghton Mifflin, 1990), 151–52, 155. **Rational operation of the intellect:** Sigmund Freud, *The Future of an Illusion*, trans. James Strachey (New York: W. W. Norton, 1969), 56. **Ludistic tendencies:** Jean Piaget, *Judgment and Reasoning in the Child*, trans. Marjorie Warden (New York: Harcourt, Brace, 1928), 202. **Awareness of more:** William James, *The Varieties of Religious Experience* (1902; repr., New York: Penguin, 1982), 58, 511. **Coles on children as soulful:** Coles, *Spiritual Life of Children*, xvii–xviii. **Julian's visions:** Julian of Norwich, *Showings*, trans. Edmund Colledge and James Walsh (Mahwah, NJ: Paulist Press, 1978), 130, 279.

Chapter 3: Logic and Imagination

Monty Python: Terry Gilliam and Terry Jones, dirs., *Monty Python and the Holy Grail* (Culver City, CA: Sony Pictures Home Entertainment, 2001), DVD. **Piaget theorized:** Piaget, *Judgment and Reasoning in the Child*. **Syllogism studies:** Maria G. Dias and Paul L. Harris, "The Effect of Make-believe Play on Deductive Reasoning," *British Journal of Developmental Psychology* 6 (1988): 207–21. Dias and Harris were motivated by an earlier study by J. Hawkins, R. D. Pea, J. Glick, and S. Scribner, "'Merds That Laugh Don't Like Mushrooms': Evidence for Deductive Reasoning by Preschoolers," *Developmental Psychology* 20, no. 4

(1984): 584–94. Like Piaget, Hawkins et al. also found that young children were poor with·syllogisms based upon premises that were empirically wrong. But they created syllogisms ("make-believe stories") for children that did not carry expectations, such as "Bangas are purple animals. Purple animals always sneeze at people. Do bangas sneeze at people?" Because children had no experience or knowledge of bangas, the question did not have an obvious answer. Young children performed significantly better than they had with incongruent syllogisms and better than chance. Children justified their answers by saying things such as "Because bangas are purple animals." By taking away the incongruence, even four-year-olds were capable of deductive, theoretical logic. **Ruby C:** Harvey, *Imaginary Playmates*, 7. **Physiological psychology:** Nathan Harvey, *Physiological Psychology* (Ypsilanti, MI: State Normal College, 1911). **Seen as vividly as living children:** Harvey, *Imaginary Playmates*, 21. **Retinal image:** The great psychologist of perception, J. J. Gibson once pointed out that much fuss is made about the retinal image in perception theory, but nobody sees the image, not even the perceiver. James Jerome Gibson, *The Senses Considered as Perceptual Systems* (Boston: Houghton Mifflin, 1966). **Svendsen study:** Margaret M. Svendsen, "Children's Imaginary Companions," *Archives of Neurology and Psychiatry* (1934): 985–99. **A collection of divergent experiences:** Harvey, *Imaginary Playmates*, 7. **No signs of pretend play until second year:** Paul Harris, *The Work of the Imagination* (Oxford: Blackwell, 2000), 27. One of Harris's main contentions is that realism comes first developmentally. For historical perspective, Harris draws upon the writings of Swiss psychiatrist Eugen Bleuler, a contemporary of Freud, to help paint an alternative to the Freudian-Piagetian developmental picture. For Bleuler, fantasy is part of everybody's thinking—in adults' dreams and reveries and in children's pretend play. Children and adults alike move back and forth between the two realms during any given day or moment. For Bleuler, babies are not born into a world of hallucination and images. Rather, the imagination is added to realistic thinking and develops with it, enabling the growing mind to entertain alternatives and possibilities in a way realism alone cannot. See Eugen Bleuler, "Autistic Thinking," in *Organization and Pathology of Thought*, ed. David Rappaport (New York: Columbia University Press, 1951), 399–437. **Visual cliff:** Eleanor Gibson and Richard D. Walk, "Visual Cliff," *Scientific American* 202 (1960): 64–71. **Intuitive physicists and psychologists:** For a fuller descriptions of babies' core knowledge and expectations, see Elizabeth S. Spelke and Katherine D. Kinzler, "Core Knowledge," *Developmental Science* 10: no. 1 (2007): 89–96; and Annette Karmiloff-Smith, *Beyond Modularity: A Developmental Perspective on Cognitive Science* (Cambridge, MA: MIT Press, 1992), ch. 5. **Pleistocene:** Allison Gopnik, *The Philosophical Baby: What Children's Minds Tell Us About Truth, Love, and the Meaning of Life* (New York: Farrar, Straus and Giroux, 2009). **Pretend spill experiment:**

Harris, *Work of the Imagination*, describes this and the popsicle stick experiment, as well as several others in chapter 2. **Double knowledge:** For more on this notion, see Alan M. Leslie, "Pretense and Representation: The Origins of Theory of Mind," *Psychological Review* 94, no. 4 (1987): 412–26. **Pretense-reality errors:** Alison Bourchier and Alyson Davis, "Children's Understanding of the Pretence-Reality Distinction: A Review of Current Theory and Evidence," *Developmental Science* 5, no. 4 (2002): 397–413. **Naturally credulous:** For more on this point, see a helpful review of reality-pretense studies by Deena Skolnick Weisberg, "Distinguishing Imagination from Reality," in *The Oxford Handbook of the Development of Imagination*, ed. Marjorie Taylor (New York: Oxford University Press, 2013), 75–93. **Vividness of mental images/studies with adults:** For a fascinating example, see Tanya M. Luhrmann, *When God Talks Back: Understanding the American Evangelical Relationship with God* (New York: Vintage, 2012). This award-winning book provides a rich description of evangelical Christian adults engaging in various practices (such as pouring coffee for God) devoted to making the experience of God feel more real, more alive and intense, precisely in light of the invisibility/intangibility of the divine. Her research is ultimately exploring the religious imaginations of adults, whereas I am exploring the earlier ground of the imagination in childhood and the ways in which it may feed the religious imagination of adulthood. ***Blue Day:*** Daniel Tammet, *Born on a Blue Day: Inside the Extraordinary Mind of an Autistic Savant* (New York/London: Free Press, 2006). **Mindblindness:** Simon Baron-Cohen, *Mindblindness: An Essay on Autism and Theory of Mind* (Cambridge, MA: MIT Press, 1997), 1. **Asperger:** Since *Born on a Blue Day* was published, the American Psychiatric Association's *Diagnostic and Statistical Manual of Mental Disorders*, 5th ed. (Arlington, VA: American Psychiatric Publishing, 2013) now identifies those who would formerly have been diagnosed with Asperger syndrome as having autism spectrum disorder. Many still use the term *Asperger's*, however. **"Stone Soup":** Tammet, *Blue Day*, 51–52. **Sandbox . . . soles:** Tammet, 18–19. **Eye contact . . . other person:** Tammet, 74–75. **Anne:** Tammet, 79. **Loneliness:** While some children may compensate for loneliness with imaginary friends, I am not convinced that we can reverse the logic—that is, if you have imaginary friends, then you must be lonely.

Chapter 4: Sharing

Joint attention: Michael Tomasello, *The Cultural Origins of Human Cognition* (Cambridge, MA: Harvard University Press, 1999), 61–70. **Complex cognitive abilities in primates:** Michael Tomasello and Josep Call, *Primate Cognition* (New York: Oxford University Press, 1997). **Chimpanzees may even cooperate:** See Frans deWaal, *Are We Smart Enough to Know How Smart Animals Are?* (New York: W. W. Norton, 2016). **Nonhuman**

primates don't point: Tomasello, *Cultural Origins of Human Cognition*, 21. There is some evidence that domesticated chimps will reach out towards an object they want from a human, but Tomasello finds no evidence for pointing in the wild. For a more recent discussion, see Michael Tomasello and Josep Call, "Thirty Years of Great Ape Gestures," *Animal Cognition* (February 2018), https://doi.org/10.1007/s10071-018-1167-1. **Original Knowing:** J. Bradley Wigger, *Original Knowing: How Religion, Science, and the Human Mind Point to the Irreducible Depth of Life* (Eugene, OR: Cascade Press, 2013). **We-mode:** Michael Tomasello, *Why We Cooperate*, Boston Review Book (Cambridge, MA: MIT Press, 2009), 63. See also Michael Tomasello, *A Natural History of Human Thinking* (Cambridge, MA: Harvard University Press, 2014). **Language in humans:** Here I mean language with structure, grammar, and recursion and not simply what's called "manipulative speech"—that is, sounds animals use to warn or attract. See Wigger, *Original Knowing*, chapter 10. **Anne's good-bye:** Tammet, *Blue Day*, 79. **Bridge to Terabithia:** Katherine Paterson, *Bridge to Terabithia* (New York: HarperCollins, 1977). **"Dorothy lived":** Frank Baum, *The Wizard of Oz* (Indianapolis: Bobbs Merrill, 1903), 12. **Stories may help train us in relationships:** See Raymond Marr and Keith Oatley, "The Function of Fiction Is the Abstraction and Simulation of Social Experience," *Perspectives on Psychological Science* 3, no. 3 (2008): 173–92. They suggest that fiction allows us to practice skills of empathy. Abstracting and compressing relevant elements of complex relationships allows the lessons learned to be more easily transferrable to life situations. The process is similar to the way an equation abstracts and summarizes features of the physical world—say, a pendulum's swing. For a good summary, see Keith Oatley, *Such Stuff as Dreams: The Psychology of Fiction* (West Sussex, UK: Wiley-Blackwell, 2011). **Invisible Ruth:** In this instance I not only changed the name of the girl but of the invisible friend as well since they share the same name. **Big bang of the mind:** William H. Calvin, *A Brief History of the Mind* (New York: Oxford University Press, 2004). See also Wigger, *Original Knowing*; and Tomasello, *Natural History of Human Thinking*, for more detail.

Chapter 5: Wild Mind

***Foster's Home*:** Craig McCracken, Craig Kellman, Rob Renzetti, and Eric Pringle, dirs., *Foster's Home for Imaginary Friends* (Atlanta, GA: Turner Home Entertainment, 2007), DVD. ***Foster's Home* comic book:** Ivan Cohen, Louise Simonson, Paulina Ganucheau, and Derek Charm, *Super Secret War! Foster's Home for Imaginary Friends* (San Diego, CA: Idea & Design Works Publishing, 2014). **Charlie Ravioli:** Adam Gopnik, "Bumping into Mr. Ravioli: A Theory of Busyness, and Its Hero," *New Yorker* (September 30, 2001): 80–

84, quote from 82. **Essence of Steveness:** Cognitive psychologists call this essentialism. See Susan Gelman, *The Essential Child: Origins of Essentialism in Everyday Thought* (New York: Oxford University Press, 2005). Essentialism in general is "the view that categories have an underlying reality or true nature that one cannot observe directly but that gives an object its identity" (3). **Skunk or raccoon:** Frank Keil, "The Acquisition of Natural Kind and Artifact Terms," in *Language, Learning and Concept Acquisition*, ed. Ausonio Marras and William Demopoulos (Norwood, NJ: Ablex, 1986), 133–53. **Cactus or porcupine:** Keil, "Acquisition of Natural Kind." See also Frank Keil, *Concepts, Kinds, and Cognitive Development* (Cambridge, MA: MIT Press, 1992). **Essentialism related to individuals:** Gelman, *Essential Child*, calls this "individual essentialism." **Underlying continuity:** Significantly, we identify continuity amidst change even in our bodily sensing of the world. The interaction of stability and change is what gives rise to stimulus information. Our bodies, even at rest, are never completely static. For example, our eyes are constantly moving in little saccades, even when it feels like we are just staring. See Gibson, *Senses Considered as Perceptual Systems*, and J. Bradley Wigger, *The Texture of Mystery: An Interdisciplinary Inquiry into Perception and Learning* (London: Associated University Presses, 1998). **I-Thou:** Martin Buber, *I and Thou* (New York: Scribner, 1958). **Proteus:** All quotes are from Homer, *The Odyssey*, trans. Robert Fitzgerald (New York: Farrar, Straus and Giroux, 1998), book IV, lines 420–630. **Sleepwalking:** Patrick McNamara, *An Evolutionary Psychology of Sleep and Dreams* (Westport, CT: Praeger, 2004). **Proteanism in animals:** See Peter Driver and David Humphries, *Protean Behavior: The Biology of Unpredictability* (Oxford: Clarendon Press, 1988). They identify and catalogue various forms of unpredictability that have served the animal world well, and I have drawn upon these descriptions for the examples of proteanism presented here. **Hillman quote:** James Hillman, *The Dream and the Underworld* (New York: Harper & Row, 1979), 80. **Play as practice for adulthood:** This theory goes back to the work of Karl Groos. See Karl Groos, Elizabeth L. Baldwin, and James Mark Baldwin, *The Play of Animals* (New York: D. Appleton, 1898). **Play in bees, sharks, zoo animals:** Gordon Burghardt, "The Comparative Reach of Play and Brain: Perspective, Evidence, and Implications," *American Journal of Play* (Winter 2010): 338–56. **Polar bear and dog:** Stuart Brown, "Play Is More than Fun," lecture, *TED* (May 2008), www.ted.com/talks/stuart_brown_says_play_is_more_than_fun_it_s_vital#t-146063. **Horses running in new fields:** These examples illustrating the creative function and emotional benefits of play are drawn from Anthony D. Pellegrini, Danielle Dupuis, and Peter K. Smith, "Play in Evolution and Development," *Developmental Review* 27, no. 2 (June 2007): 261–76.

Chapter 6: Who Knows What?

"Theory of Mind": Taylor, *Imaginary Companions*, 47. **New York Times article:** Robin
Marantz Henig, "Darwin's God," *New York Times Magazine*, March 4, 2007, www.nytimes.
com/2007/03/04/magazine/04evolution.t.html. **Playing in theory of mind:** See M. Leslie, "Pretense and Representation." **Surprising-contents test:** Justin L. Barrett, Rebekah
A. Richert, and Amanda Driesenga, "God's Beliefs versus Mother's: The Development
of Nonhuman Agent Concepts," *Child Development* 72 (2001): 50–65. It could be that
knowledge of the actual contents of the box overrides the judgment of younger children in
what's called a *reality bias*. **Perspective-taking experiments:** Jean Piaget and Bärbel Inhel-
der, *The Child's Conception of Space*, trans. F. J. Langdon and J. L. Lunzer (New York: W. W.
Norton, 1956). **Raisin box test:** Marjorie Taylor and Stephanie M. Carlson, "The Relation
between Individual Differences in Fantasy and Theory of Mind," *Child Development* 68
(1997): 436–55. While they found this effect among four-year-olds, they did not find it
among three-year-olds. They conclude, "Our intuition is that extensive fantasy experiences
help children develop an understanding of mind" (452). For a more recent study, see Marta
Giménez-Dasí, Francisco Pons, and Patrick K. Bender, "Imaginary Companions, Theory
of Mind and Emotion Understanding in Young Children," *European Early Childhood Education Research Journal* 24, no. 2 (2016): 186–97. They found a similar pattern among
children in Spain. In our research, we never had enough children of any particular age (by
year) with IFs to be able to meaningfully compare children with and without IFs. Even
so, in Malawi (discussed in the next chapter), when grouping the five- and six-year-olds
together, the pass rate in a false-belief test was 76 percent for the 13 children with IFs and
45 percent for those without (53 children). The difference is indeed statistically significant.
[A chi-square test for goodness of fit yielded χ^2 *(1, N = 66)* = 1.69, *p* = .041.] But I am
cautious. One or two misunderstandings could easily have yielded different, nonsignificant
statistical results. To date, the finding has not been subjected to peer review—another
reason for caution. Nonetheless, when combined with the other two studies, children at a
threshold age for understanding false belief (in Malawi, five- and six-year-olds) do not seem
to be hindered by their imaginative play and may be helped by it when it comes to understanding minds. **"Fifteen years ago" quote:** Justin Barrett, "Cognitive Science of Religion:
What Is It and Why Is It?" *Religion Compass* 1, no. 6 (2007): 768–86. **God as big person
in the sky:** Jean Piaget, *The Child's Conception of the World*, trans. Joan Tomlinson and
Andrew Tomlinson (London: Routledge and Kegan Paul, 1929). **Some beliefs may come
more easily:** Justin L. Barrett, *Why Would Anyone Believe in God?* (Walnut Creek, CA: Al-
tamira Press, 2004). For a more recent discussion, including cross-cultural comparisons, see

Justin L. Barrett, "Religion Is Kid's Stuff: Minimally Counterintuitive Concepts Are Better Remembered by Young People," in *Religious Cognition in China: "Homo Religiosus" and the Dragon*, ed. Ryan G. Hornbeck, Justin L. Barrett, and Madeline Kang (Cham, Switz.: Springer International, 2017), 125–38. **Barrett asked *New York Times* interviewer:** Henig, "Darwin's God." **Zeman on consciousness:** Adam Zeman, *Consciousness: A User's Guide* (New Haven, CT: Yale University Press, 2002). **US communes study:** Richard Sosis and Eric R. Bressler, "Cooperation and Commune Longevity: A Test of the Costly Signaling Theory of Religion," *Cross-Cultural Research* 37, no. 2 (2003): 211–39. **Kibbutzim study:** Richard Sosis and Bradley J. Ruffle, "Religious Ritual and Cooperation: Testing for a Relationship on Israeli Religious and Secular Kibbutzim," *Current Anthropology* 44, no. 5 (2003): 713–22. **Three different theory-of-mind tasks:** This study is more fully described and analyzed in J. Bradley Wigger, Katrina Paxson, and Lacey Ryan, "What Do Invisible Friends Know? Imaginary Companions, God, and Theory of Mind," *International Journal for the Psychology of Religion* 23 no. 1 (2013): 2–14. **God as an agent:** The children came from a variety of Christian denominations and none said anything like "Who is God?" **Occluded-picture study:** While 63 percent of the children claimed they knew what the whole picture was before it was revealed to them, only 53 percent thought their best friend would know, 44 percent said a dog would know, and an overwhelming number of children (90 percent) said that God would know the whole picture. Imaginary friends were slightly more likely to know (67 percent) than everyone except God. By themselves the scores are not a proper theory-of-mind measure because children were guessing about something they saw and figured their best friends, if not dogs, could guess too. They did not yet know what they did not know. Alone, it did not measure theory-of-mind development because, except for answers for the dog, age did not show statistically significant differences. Older and younger children alike thought they could figure out what the whole picture was. So the bigger question was how the children would answer when they realized their own guesses were wrong—that is, when they saw the whole picture. **"Mr. Smart knows everything":** Jonathan D. Lane, Henry M. Wellman, and E. Margaret Evans, "Children's Understanding of Ordinary and Extraordinary Minds," *Child Development* 81, no. 5 (2010): 1475–89. **Natural to attribute special powers:** Barrett, in *Why Would Anyone Believe in God*, points to the role of religious education (Sunday school and Bible stories that tell of an extraordinary character called God) as well. But the assumption had been that it is difficult for children to really comprehend these stories or the implications about God's special powers, especially since they are about a figure children only hear about and never see. But religious education alone is likely only part of the story. Just as it is difficult for humans to think or speak meaningfully in binary code (rather than in English or Swahili), religious education would likely flounder if children's minds were not prepared to differentiate various types of minds, including an extraordinary one like God's. Justin Barrett and Rebekah Richert, "Anthropomorphism or Preparedness? Exploring Children's God Concepts," *Review of Religious Research* 44 (2003): 300–312, proposes an alternative to the notion that children necessarily base the understanding of the minds of others—whether animals or gods—on a human model. Instead, in what they call the *preparedness hypothesis*, children are ready to think about various types of minds, including extraordinary ones, at ages much younger than Piaget believed. That is, children's understanding of other minds may be quite flexible, capable of something more fine-tuned than crude concreteness and rigid assumptions. For possible cross-cultural evidence of the preparedness hypothesis, see Tyler S. Greenway, Gregory S. Foley, Brianna C. Nystrum, and Justin L. Barrett, "Dogs, Santa Claus, and Sun Wukong: Children's Understanding of Nonhuman Minds," in *Religious Cognition in China: "Homo Religiosus" and the Dragon*, ed. Ryan G. Hornbeck, Justin L. Barrett, and Madeleine Kang (Cham, Switz.: Springer International, 2017), 97–109. **Mayan study:** Nicola Knight, "Yukatek Maya Children's Attributions of Belief to Natural and Non-Natural Entities," *Journal of Cognition and Culture* 8 (2008): 235–43.

Chapter 7: Ancestors and Angels

Children in India: Antonia A. Mills, "Are Children with Imaginary Playmates and Children Said to Remember Previous Lives Cross-culturally Comparable Categories?," *Transcultural Psychiatry* 40 (2003): 67–90, quotes from 67. **Babbling:** Alison Gopnik, Andrew N. Meltzoff, and Patricia K. Kuhl, *The Scientist in the Crib: What Early Learning Tells Us about the Mind* (New York: Harper, 1999), 110–11. See also Michael Tomasello, *Constructing a Language: A Usage-Based Theory of Language Acquisition* (Cambridge, MA: Harvard University Press, 2003), 31ff. **Luo culture:** Denis Oluoch-Oduor, in discussion with the author, May 25, 2012. See also Nancy Schwartz, "Active Dead or Alive: Some Kenyan Views about the Agency of Luo and Luyia Women Pre- and Post-mortem," *Journal of Religion in Africa* 30, no. 4 (2000): 433–67; and Parker Shipton, "Debts and Trespasses: Land, Mortgages, and the Ancestors in Western Kenya," *Africa: Journal of the International African Institute* 62 no. 3 (1992): 357–88. **Green Belt Movement:** For more, see www.greenbeltmovement. org. **Environment as sacred:** Wangari Maathai, *Replenishing the Earth: Spiritual Values for Healing Ourselves and the World* (New York: Doubleday, 2010), 143. **Interviewed one hundred Luo children:** A more detailed description of the IF portion of the interviews in the four non-US countries, along with the results can be found in Wigger, "Invisible Friends across Four Countries." **Contingencies affecting rates of IFs:** See Appendix. **Orthodox children in Greece study:** Nikolaos Makris and Dimitris Pnevmatikos, "Children's Understanding of Human and Super-natural Mind," *Cognitive Development* 22 (2007): 365–75. Older children (over five years) said in each case a puppet would not know the contents but God would. Subsequent research shows a similar pattern to the Greek study. See Florian Kiessling and Josef Perner, "God–Mother–Baby: What Children Think They Know," *Child Development* (2013), https://doi.org/10.1111/cdev.12210; and Lane, Wellman, and Evans, "Children's Understanding of Ordinary and Extraordinary Minds." **Executive function and theory of mind:** See Mark A. Sabbagh, Fen Xu, Stephanie M. Carlson, Louis J. Moses, and Kang Lee, "The Development of Executive Functioning and Theory of Mind: A Comparison of Chinese and U.S. Preschoolers," *Psychological Science* 17, no. 1 (2006): 74–81. **Passing knowledge-ignorance test before false-belief:** G.-Juergen Hogrefe, Heinz Wimmer, and Josef Perner, "Ignorance versus False Belief: A Developmental Lag in Attribution of Epistemic States," *Child Development* 57 (1986): 567–82. **Nonhumans understanding ignorance:** Josep Call and Michael Tomasello, "Does the Chimpanzee Have a Theory of Mind? 30 Years Later," *Trends in Cognitive Sciences* 12, no. 5 (May, 2008): 187–92. **Muslims as likely as Christians:** Forty-five of the children were Muslim (20 percent). Of them, thirteen (29 percent) claimed an invisible friend, slightly higher than the rate for Christian children (25 percent), but like gender, not statistically significant. **Not statistically significant:** If you are not a reader of science journals or have ever wondered what *significance* means in relation to statistics, the basic idea is that the rate difference is not large enough to rule out the ordinary and random variations that happen among samples. For example, imagine that I interviewed children in Winnipeg, Canada, and found that 40 percent of the boys had imaginary friends, but only 20 percent of the girls had one. That would seem like a big difference and it would be tempting to claim that Canadian boys are twice as likely as Canadian girls to have invisible friends. The difference would indeed be significant had I interviewed 220 children in Winnipeg. But what if I had interviewed only ten children: five girls and five boys? The rate difference would be based upon finding two boys among the five (40 percent) with imaginary friends and one girl (20 percent) with an imaginary friend. We can easily imagine that someone else interviewing ten other children in Winnipeg could easily find the reverse: two girls and one boy having invisible friends. So statisticians have developed a discipline for calculating the point at which we can be more confident that some factor or factors other than random variations are occurring. Of course this is an oversimplified explanation, but I hope it may be helpful to those unfamiliar with statistical significance. **Spirits instead** of ancestors in Malawi: Due to high rates of disease and poverty, many of the children interviewed were orphans and may have had less knowledge about their own ancestors.

Chapter 8: Gods and Godsibbs

Research in Nepal: Approval for conducting this research was granted by the Nepal Health Research Council of the federal government. Religion in Nepal: According to the latest census, the nation is 81 percent Hindu and 9 percent Buddhist, with no other religious tradition representing more than 5 percent. *National Population and Housing Census* (Kathmandu: Government of Nepal, Central Bureau of Statistics, 2012). Pari: See David Templeman, "Iranian Themes in Tibetan Tantric Culture: The Dakini," in *Religion and Secular Culture in Tibet: Tibetan Studies II*, ed. Henk Blezer (London: Brill, 2002), 113–28. See also D. L. R. Lorimer and Emily Overend Lorimer, *Persian Tales* (London: Macmillan, 1919). High season of make-believe: Singer and Singer, *House of Make-Believe*, 64. Taylor and Carlson study of parental attitudes: Marjorie Taylor and Stephanie M. Carlson, "The Influence of Religious Beliefs on Parental Attitudes about Children's Fantasy Behavior," in *Imagining the Impossible: Magical, Scientific, and Religious Thinking in Children*, ed. Karl S. Rosengren, Carl N. Johnson, and Paul Harris (Cambridge, UK: Cambridge University Press, 2000). Case of imaginary friends in Nepal remains open: For more about the varying rates of IFs between countries, see Wigger, "Invisible Friends across Four Countries," which draws upon the work of Suzanne Gaskins, "Pretend Play as Culturally Constructed Activity," in *Oxford Handbook of the Development of Imagination*, ed. Marjorie Taylor (New York: Oxford University Press, 2013), 224–47. Gaskins speculates that some cultures support imaginative play, some tolerate it, and some discourage it. Thirteen different deities: A few children were either unsure or could not remember the name of the deity they were thinking of, saying something like, "I can see it in the temple, but can't remember." The most often named deities were Shiva (16 percent), Buddha (14 percent), Ganesh (13 percent), and Parvati (12 percent), constituting over half of the responses. Comparison between countries: For a full analysis of the IF rates and comparisons, see Wigger, "Invisible Friends across Four Countries." As far as I can find as I write, this is the first and only cross-cultural study of invisible friends that used the same interview technique with each sample. DR as overwhelmingly Christian: "Religion in Latin America," Pew Research Center, November 13, 2014, www.pewforum. org/2014/11/13/religion-in-latin-america/#. While the majority of Dominicans are Roman Catholic, the children we interviewed attended Protestant-sponsored schools and were a mix of Protestant and Catholic. Friend of God: Abraham is called a friend of God in the book of James (2:23); the Wisdom of Solomon quote comes from 7:27 (*New Revised Standard*

Version Bible [New York: National Council of the Churches of Christ in the United States of America, 1989]). **Erikson on trust versus mistrust:** Erik H. Erikson, *Childhood and Society* (New York: W. W. Norton, 1950). **Santa Claus in the DR:** Originally, instead of Santa, we planned to ask children about the Magi, or "wise men," of the Christmas story. Traditionally in the DR, the Magi were the ones to bring gifts on Epiphany, reflecting how the Magi brought gifts to baby Jesus. But in piloting the interview with Dominican children, only some of them knew about the Magi, but they all knew Santa. It probably speaks to the power and influence of marketing and mass media on cultures outside the US over the past few decades. **IFs as in-betweens in DR:** Of the thirty-four children with imaginary friends, half or more attributed special knowledge to them: 50 percent in the knowledge-ignorance (closed bag) task and 58 percent in the false-belief (matchbox) task. **Deep cognitive bias:** Cognitive biases and tendencies intersect with particular cultures, with varied languages, social practices, and teachings that could affect how children think about the minds and knowledge of others. In other words, humans may have strong mental tendencies just as we have physical tendencies (for example, attraction to sweet or salty foods), but there are both cultural variations (different types of candies and desserts) as well as individual variation (preference for salty foods over sweets). **Dunbar on gossip:** Robin Dunbar is an evolutionary psychologist who studies the communication patterns of primates. See Robin Dunbar, *Grooming, Gossip, and the Evolution of Language* (Cambridge, MA: Harvard University Press, 1996). **Godsibb:** "Gossip," *OED Online*, Oxford University Press, 2016, www.oed.com. **Gossip as grooming:** Robin I. M. Dunbar, "Gossip in Evolutionary Perspective." *Review of General Psychology* 8, no. 2 (2004): 100–110. According to Dunbar, roughly two-thirds of our talk is devoted to social concerns. While humans still employ some grooming, talk is more efficient since we can communicate with more than one person at a time and information does not have to be limited to the here and now. Talk can refer to third parties to help us keep track of others, either those in an alliance (friends and family) or those who threaten them. As Dunbar puts it, "Language allows us to seek out what has been going on behind our backs. Indeed, we can even be proactive about it and tell our friends and relations what we have seen when we think it might be in their interests to know" (103). *Eccentric* **from Greek:** *OED Online*. I am loosely drawing upon a philosophical tradition that describes human existence as exocentric: open to the world, grounded beyond ourselves. See, for example, Max Scheler, *Man's Place in Nature*, trans. Hans Meyerhoff (New York: Noonday Press, 1961); and Wolfhart Pannenberg, *Anthropology in Theological Perspective*, trans. Matthew J. O'Connell (Philadelphia: Westminster Press, 1985).

Chapter 9: Original Knowing

DNA analyses: See Tomasello, *Cultural Origins of Human Cognition*. See also "Genetics: What Does It Mean to be Human?," Smithsonian National Museum of Natural History, August 25, 2017, http://humanorigins.si.edu/evidence/genetics. **Time problem:** Tomasello, *Cultural Origins of Human Cognition*, 2. This issue is at the heart of Wigger, *Original Knowing*, especially part 4. Here, I am summarizing the argument in relation to imagination, which was not emphasized as much in that work. **Jaynes quote:** Julian Jaynes, *The Origin of Consciousness in the Breakdwon of the Bicameral Mind* (Boston: Houghton Mifflin, 1990), 1. **Natalie quote:** Coles, *Spiritual Life of Children*, 155. **Toolmaking:** For more detail about the evolution of toolmaking and the kind of mind that generates it, see Wigger, *Original Knowing*, especially chapter 5. Much of this discussion is indebted to the research and writing of Michael Tomasello. **Rake experiment:** Katherine Nagell, Kelly Jaakkola, and Michael Tomasello, "Processes of Social Learning in the Tool Use of Chimpanzees (*Pan troglodytes*) and Human Children (*Homo sapiens*)," *Journal of Comparative Psychology* 107 (1993): 174–86. **Three buckets experiment:** Michael Tomasello, Malinda Carpenter, Josep Call, Tany Behne, and Henrike Moll, "Understanding and Sharing Intentions: The Origins of Cultural Cognition," *Behavioral and Brain Sciences* 28 (2005): 675–735, quote from 724. A similar study tried to determine whether it mattered that the pointer was human. They trained a chimpanzee to point on command, but the results were no better than they were with a human pointing. Shoji Itakura, Bryan Agnetta, Brian Hare, and Michael Tomasello, "Chimpanzee Use of Human and Conspecific Social Cues to Locate Hidden Food," *Developmental Science* 2, no. 4 (1999): 448–56. **Carrying a log:** As one research article (Tomasello et al., "Understanding and Sharing Intentions") observes, after hundreds of primate studies, "it is almost unimaginable that two chimpanzees might spontaneously do something as simple as carry something heavy together or make a tool together" (685). **Sin and evil:** For more concerning my take on this theological tradition, see J. Bradley Wigger, *The Power of God at Home* (San Francisco: Jossey-Bass, 2003), especially chapters 4 and 5. **Moral philosophers:** See Buber, *I and Thou*; Gabriel Marcel, *The Mystery of Being*, trans. G. S. Fraser (Lanham, MD: University Press of America, 1950); Emmanuel Levinas, *Totality and Infinity: An Essay on Exteriority*, trans. Alphonso Lingis (Dordrecht, Neth.: Kluwer Academic, 1991). **Wonder/radical amazement quotes:** Abraham Joshua Heschel, *Man Is Not Alone: A Philosophy of Religion* (New York: Farrar, Straus, and Giroux, 1951), 65, 13.

Chapter 10: Friends of God

Orsi quote: Robert A. Orsi, *Between Heaven and Earth: The Religious Worlds People Make and the Scholars Who Study Them* (Princeton, NJ: Princeton University Press, 2005), 2. **Dionne on characters:** Karen Dionne, "When Characters Talk, Writers Listen," Huffington Post, March 19, 2014, accessed August 25, 2017, www.huffingtonpost.com/karen-dionne/when-characters-talk-writ_b_4993933.html. **Inner Voices project:** Writers' Inner Voices, "Introduction to Writers Inner Voices Writers' Inner Voices," June 4, 2014, https://writersinnervoices.com. **Rosenblatt on writing:** Roger Rosenblatt, "The Invisible Forces That Make Writing Work," Book Review, *New York Times*, August 25, 2017, www.nytimes.com/2017/08/25/books/review/roger-rosenblatt-writing-invisible.html. **Sontag on writing:** Susan Sontag, *As Consciousness Is Harnessed to Flesh: Journals and Notebooks, 1964–1980*, ed. David Rieff (New York: Farrar, Straus and Giroux, 2012), 38. **Bering on God illusion:** Jesse Bering, *The Belief Instinct: The Psychology of Souls, Destiny, and the Meaning of Life* (New York: W. W. Norton, 2011), 37. **Something rather than nothing:** Jim Holt, *Why Does the World Exist? An Existential Detective Story* (New York: W. W. Norton, 2012) does a marvelous job laying out the multiple reasons both atheism and theism wrestle with the question. **"Nasty suspicion" in theology:** Edward Farley, *Ecclesial Man: A Social Phenomenology of Faith and Reality* (Philadelphia: Fortress, 1975), 6. **Tillich on courage:** Paul Tillich, *The Courage to Be* (New Haven, CT: Yale University Press, 1952), 165. **Luhrmann research:** Tanya M. Luhrmann, *When God Talks Back: Understanding the American Evangelical Relationship with God* (New York: Vintage, 2012); quotes from xii–xiii, 74. **Brother Lawrence quotes:** Brother Lawrence, *The Practice of the Presence of God* (Old Tappan, NJ: Fleming H. Revell, 1958), 34–36, 29. **Yihudim:** Lawrence Fine, *Physician of the Soul, Healer of the Cosmos: Isaac Luria and His Kabbalistic Fellowship* (Stanford, CA: Stanford University Press, 2003), ch. 8. **Tsimtsum:** The description of *tsimtsum* is drawn from Fine, *Physician of the Soul*, ch. 4. Luria himself wrote very little, but he taught much, and his students wrote about his teachings. Fine's book is an excellent source for exploring the complexities of Luria's thought and influence on the community in Safed as well as Jewish mysticism in general.

INDEX

Ames, Louise Bates, 216–17
ancestor (spirits): Hopi, 40, 46–47, 178;
    Kenyan (Luo), 127–28, 130–133,
    138, 147, 178; Malawian, 144. *See also*
    spirits
angels: as agents in theory-of-mind tests,
    110, 144–45, 157, 170; as figures in
    religions, 6, 122, 155, 199, 206; as
    invisible friends, 29–30
anthropomorphism, 229
arux/alux, 122–24
Auden, W. H., 8, 221
autism, 61–62, 129, 224

Baron-Cohen, Simon, 61, 224
Barrett, Justin: and cognitive science of
    religion, 109–13, 227, 29; and theory
    of mind, 106, 109–10, 116, 120–21,
    227–29
Bering, Jesse, 199–200, 234
Bleuler, Eugen, 223
Bouldin, Paula, 216, 218
Brown, Stuart, 98, 226

Buber, Martin, 92, 226, 233
Buddhism, 150, 153–54, 157, 231
Buechner, Frederick, 25–26, 195, 222
Burnstein, M., 216–17

Call, Josep, 224–25, 230, 233
Calvin, William, 79, 225
Calvin and Hobbes (comic strip), 19–20,
    97, 129
Carlson, Stephanie, 155, 216, 218, 227,
    230–31
Carroll, Lewis (Charles Dodgson), 1, 111,
    113, 116, 221
Carvalhaes, Cláudio, 194, 204–5
children interviewed (Christian): in the
    DR, 162, 231; Greek Orthodox,
    137, 231; in Kenya, 130, 132, 147;
    in Malawi, 140–42, 147, 230; in
    Nepal, 150, 154, 157; Protestant, 231;
    Roman Catholic, 122, 231; in the US,
    7, 127, 155, 228
children interviewed (Hindu), 151–57. *See
    also* Nepal

 SPIRITUAL PHENOMENA